D0769027

THE
PRIVATIZATION
OF POLICING

Two Views

Controversies in Public Policy

edited by
Rita J. Simon

THE PRIVATIZATION OF POLICING

Two Views

Brian Forst
Peter K. Manning

GEORGETOWN UNIVERSITY PRESS / WASHINGTON, D.C.

HOUSTON PUBLIC LIBRARY

R01135 73619

Georgetown University Press, Washington, D.C.
©1999 by Georgetown University Press. All rights reserved
Printed in the United States of America

10 9 8 7 6 5 4 3 2 1   1999

THIS VOLUME IS PRINTED ON ACID-FREE OFFSET BOOK PAPER

Library of Congress Cataloging-in-Publication Data
Forst, Brian.
    The privatization of policing : two views / Brian Forst, P.K.
Manning
        p. m. — (Controversies in public policy)
    Includes index.
    ISBN 0-87840-734-0 (cloth). — ISBN 0-87840-735-9 (pbk.)
    1. Criminal justice, Administration of—United States.
2. Privatization—United States. 3. Police—Contracting out—United
States. 4. Police—United States. 5. Law enforcement—United
States. I. Manning, Peter K. II. Title. III. Series.
HV9950.F67 1999
363.2'0973—dc21   99-18789
                                                        CIP

Contents

Preface

The Privatization of Policing is the sixth volume in a pro and con series on important public issues, and the first to be published by Georgetown University Press. Other issues that were debated in earlier volumes include abortion, drugs, immigration, school vouchers, and affirmative action. As in the other volumes in this series, the authors draw upon empirical data to strengthen their analysis and support their positions. The authors debating the privatization of policing, more than the contributors to most of the other volumes, have radically different writing styles and use language quite differently. Manning has the clearly more flamboyant style, engaging in dramaturgy and use of metaphors; by contrast, Forst writes in the more straightforward yeomanlike manner of a traditional social scientist. But more than style distinguishes their positions.

They hold significantly different views, not only on the privatization of policing but on the broader issue of privatization of law enforcement, corrections and other traditionally publicly financed and controlled activities. Peter Manning is clearly suspicious and hostile toward economic theory and managerial practices. He believes that the economic issues of efficiency, and effectiveness and, indeed, the overall "free market" paradigm, are both inconsistent and harmful to the traditional police mandate which, in his view, is rooted in coercion and violence and must be controlled by the state.

Brian Forst presents a more moderate position and argues that neither public nor private policing should have or is likely to have a monopoly on law enforcement activities as we move into the twenty-first century. Focusing on the public's need for security, Forst predicts an even more varied mix of public and private police activities than are currently available, pointing out that since wealthy communities and neighborhoods have always had the option of hiring and maintaining private police protection, it is in the poorer neighborhoods that we are likely to see changes in the type and quality of law enforcement. Those changes may take the form of public subsidies to neighborhood organizations to hire private security, the formation of citizens' groups that serve voluntarily to protect the areas in which they live, or the hiring of security guards to protect commercial interests in poorer neighborhoods. In Forst's view, the twenty-first century will see significant changes in the social organization, economic control, types of activities, and characteristics of persons who perform law enforcement activities. For Brian Forst, the free market paradigm and economic incentives do not carry the stigma and fears that they hold for Peter Manning.

When you have finished reading both sections and each author's response to the other, you can decide who has made the more legitimate argument and whose picture of policing is more likely to prevail in the twenty-first century.

Rita J. Simon

Preface

The coauthors of this book come to the topic at hand with considerable interest and with perhaps more than the customary amount of trepidation. We have both devoted much of our careers to thinking about policing; we also share a strong interest in questions about privatization. And though we arrive at the topic from different paths and with different perspectives, we each respect the prior work of the other and embrace the prospect that a treatment of the subject that combines those differences is bound to be more comprehensive, more interesting, and more useful than one that does not. Though some repetition in the presenting of facts is inevitable, so, too, is the likelihood that we will interpret them somewhat differently. Vive la différence!

In an era of cross-fire television debates and in-your-face, fifteen-second sound bites, however, it is all too tempting to forsake such civilities and engage instead in the show business of strident adversarial encounter. The working title for this project, "Public v. Private Law Enforcement," suggested the latter approach more nearly than it did the former — a primary source of our initial trepidation, as we quickly experienced discomfort about any inducements to quarrel. Moreover, we found the term "law enforcement" unnecessarily restrictive, viewing the term "policing" as one that offers a richer framework for contemplation about the private and public domains of what police do.

We were confronted also with the question of format, especially, the choice of whether to simply present our respective views on the subject and leave it at that or to follow up with comments on each other's essays and perhaps a rejoinder to the comments. After reviewing each other's contributions, we decided to prepare comments designed to highlight major points of agreement and disagreement, with attempts to reconcile the most significant differences. We are comfortable with the resulting structure: a discourse, not an alley fight. We hope that most of you will conclude that the end product adds up to no less than the sum of the parts.

Brian Forst
Peter K. Manning
May 1998

Acknowledgments

Peter Manning wishes to thank Rita Simon for editorial guidance and advice; Brian Forst for cooperation and patience; the director of the School of Criminal Justice, Merry Morash, for encouragement and relief from some teaching duties; Maynard Anderson, Defense Personnel Security Research Center Director Jim Riedel, and Ted Sarbin for intellectual encouragement; the former Director of PERSEREC, Roger Denk, for jokes in the hallway and financial support; and Lynn Mattice, former director of security for Whirlpool, for funding a study of private security. Jessica Lee gathered material used throughout the book. Patricia Schramm Murphy organized materials, made phone calls, and was always cheerful and helpful. Thanks, Trish.

Peter Manning
East Lansing
May, 1999

Brian Forst wishes to thank Richard Bennett, Daniel Dreisbach, Judith Forst, James Lynch, Michael Planty, Rita Simon, and Ross Swope for their helpful comments on earlier drafts.

Brian Forst
Washington, D.C.
May, 1999

PART ONE

Brian Forst
Policing with Legitimacy, Equity, and Efficiency

❏ INTRODUCTION

A joke from the late Soviet era has a pollster asking an American, a Pole, and a Russian: "What is your opinion about the beef shortage?" The American responds, "What is 'shortage'?" The Pole responds, "What is 'beef'?" And the Russian responds, "What is 'opinion'?"[1] Clearly, a first task of inquiry is to define the terms at issue.

One can respond similarly to the question "What is your view of the privatization of policing?" by asking, "What, precisely, is meant by 'privatization,' what by 'policing,' and what by 'view'?" *Privatization* occurs typically on both the revenue-raising side and the spending-and-production side, but it can exist on the latter side alone. When it occurs on both sides, private citizens or institutions raise the funds for services that might otherwise be provided publicly and determine how they will be allocated; this includes a myriad of self-help approaches to protecting private property and personal safety. When it occurs on the spending-and-production side alone, federal, state, or local governments may contract with private sources for specific services, or private citizens or institutions may receive individualized spending authority, as in the case of food stamps or school vouchers. The range of choices made, the range and quality of services received, and the distribution of both choices and services will depend on the nature of the privatization.

Similarly, *policing* can entail a countless assortment of functions and services, ranging from conventional law enforcement responses to crime in the form of criminal investigation and arrest to crime prevention activities and attempts to improve more general "quality of life" aspects of the community. Policing has been defined generally in terms of its domestic peacekeeping role. A core distinguishing characteristic has been identified by Egon Bittner (1970): In the domestic domain, the police alone are given the authority to use nonnegotiably coercive force.[2] Beyond such distinguishing characteristics, however, the history of policing reveals varied patterns of emphasis on solving crimes, preventing them, and providing other services; I consider those in the next section, with an eye toward the respective roles of the public and private sectors during various stages in the evolution of modern policing.

Views of the role of privatization in policing are as varied as policing itself. One can take a descriptive or a prescriptive view, focusing on what is and has been or on what should be. One can take the view of a particular discipline, such as that of the political scientist, sociologist, anthropologist, or economist, or of any of the widely diverse perspective within each of those rather broad disciplines. One can further focus on matters of distribution or equity, on matters of efficiency or effectiveness, or on matters of freedom and choice; in addressing each of these matters, one can measure the quantity and quality of services delivered in any of several ways.

My approach to addressing issues of justice policy generally is eclectic, leaning more toward the economic and utilitarian than toward the perspectives of political science, history, sociology, or anthropology. Each discipline brings something important to the discussion, and I do not presume to be able to offer a comprehensive account from any one of them exclusively. The next section will take a descriptive, historical perspective: What has been the nature of policing and the role of privatization over the past millennium? The section after that will take a more prescriptive view, considering the relative strengths and weaknesses of public and private policing services, respectively. The concluding section will consider the mix of public and private policing services that appears appropriately suited to deal with the policing problems of the coming millennium, focusing on the next twenty five years or so.

❏ WHAT IS POLICING? A HISTORICAL PERSPECTIVE

Early Protection Systems

Policing, like most functions of modern government, was once exclusively in the domain of private enterprise. The policing of homicides in ancient Athens, unlike that of later times and places, was primarily a family matter; entry into the security market was restricted, and individuals without families were not well protected (Posner 1981, 223–24). The origins of modern policing are commonly attributed to England, where, prior to the Norman Conquest in 1066, men rallied to the defense of the village by raising a hue and cry when criminal behavior was evident. Variations on such basic practices were common to most other cultures as well, typically followed by tribunals that determined sanctions that would apply to the offender: public humiliation, torture, banishment, or death. From 1066 until the thirteenth century, the policing function in England was supervised under the pledge (or "frankpledge") system by a constable, who delegated to "tythings" the primary responsibility for responding to crime — generally, ten families to a tything and ten tythings to a constable. An entire tything could be harshly fined by the constable if any member of the group failed to perform his duty. Within each English county ("shire"), the constables reported to a sheriff ("reeve"). The roles of constable and sheriff represent the beginnings of a public policing function.

The pledge system gave way to the "watch system" in English towns during the thirteenth century. Local metropolitan justice systems developed around a justice of the peace (precursor to the modern judge), a constable, his assistants, and night watchmen. Thus, the policing function was organized early on within the judicial branch of government.

The Growth of Cities and the Need for Urban Protection

The Industrial Revolution attracted many thousands of people into factory towns and cities in the late eighteenth and early nineteenth centuries, creating a great need for police protection — the watch system and Britain's predominantly private, loosely organized "Associations for the Prosecution of Felons" (Elliott 1991) proved unable to respond adequately to the new demands imposed by these developments. Sir Robert Peel, Secretary of the Home Office, is generally credited with fashioning a strong public response; he created the forerunner to the modern urban police department following passage of the London Metropolitan Police Act of 1829. His design for the London Metropolitan Police Department (MPD) was modeled largely on the writings of Jeremy Bentham and others who argued for a force of peace officers (who later became known as "bobbies," in tribute to Peel) to prevent crime. Though the MPD had its occasional corrupt officer, it replaced a system of far more corrupt constables and their henchmen with carefully selected officers trained in restraint and outfitted in quasi-military navy blue uniforms, committed to serving the public twenty four hours each day (Uchida 1993, 2; Manning 1995, 378).

Thus, the British had created an institution that was squarely in the public domain. The source of the MPD's power was the English Constitution; the officers behavior was determined by rules of law (Uchida 1993).

The Rise of Policing in the United States

The United States was much slower to adopt an effective public policing service. In colonial America crimes were handled in the countryside by a fee-for-service sheriff, who was paid per criminal caught, subpoena served, and tax dollar collected. Towns used a fee-for-service system as well to pay constables working for the court to serve subpoenas and make arrests; the constable, in turn, hired and delegated responsibilities to a team of night watchmen. Meanwhile, as the West expanded, cattle theft and other crimes were handled either by a quasi-public hired marshal or by private "vigilance committees," or "vigilantes."

In the nineteenth and early twentieth centuries, immigrants from Ireland, Germany, and Italy poured into U.S. cities. The population of New York City soared from 33,000 in 1790 to some 150,000 by 1830. Race riots followed, with major upheavals in New York in 1834, Philadelphia in 1837, and St. Louis in 1850. The prevailing system of constables and night watchmen before long proved itself to be incapable of dealing with such large-scale urban crises. Militiamen were used to contain many of these disturbances, with limited success.

With more people came more serious crime and more vice, and the militia had not been created to deal with such urban matters. Our cities responded by looking across the Atlantic to shape some semblance of Peel's more effective MPD. The Boston Police Department came up with a superficial imitation of the London MPD model in 1838, less than a decade after Peel's creation, and similar models were set up in New York in 1844 and Philadelphia in 1854. These departments grew substantially during the course of the nineteenth century. While the U.S. population more than doubled from the 1860s to the early 1900s, the population of police officers more than tripled: from 1.3 officers per thousand residents in the mid-1860s to 2 officers per thousand residents by 1908 (Monkkonen 1992, 554).

Unfortunately, the similarities between the London MPD and the U.S. counterparts were primarily in form, not substance. London's officers were civil servants created by the British Constitution, sworn to keeping peace by peaceful means. Police departments in the United States hired their officers locally through a system of ward bosses operating under mayoral patronage (the U.S. Constitution makes no mention of police). Municipal police in the United States were thus free to operate with considerably more informal discretion and less formal authority than Peel's officers. They were not afforded the training, effective supervision, or job security that came with policing in the MPD of London; they were typically let go when their ward chief or mayor was not reelected. Both systems were public, but they were decidedly different from one another.

Incompetence, Corruption and Brutality

Not surprisingly, the U.S. system of municipal policing developed into one in which police were inclined to patrol the election facilities to help secure the reelection of their patrons, more in some cities than in others. The police also established reputations for being especially tough on recent immigrants and minorities. Before too long, policing in most large cities became associated with incompetence, corruption, and brutality. Despite receiving salaries about double the level of the average factory worker in 1880, they routinely took payoffs from saloonkeepers, pimps, and gamblers in return for selective nonenforcement, and from peddlers and small businesses — free meals from restaurant owners became the norm in many areas — in exchange for protection. It soon became evident that navy blue uniforms alone did not make for either integrity or effectiveness.

These early police departments were nonetheless quite different from the constable and watch systems they replaced, and in some ways better suited to deal with the problems that accompanied urbanization. They were organized in hierarchies, with military-like command and control systems as technology permitted, and with telegraph systems linking precincts to central headquarters in the 1850s and call boxes on the streets by 1867. The police were moved from the judicial to the executive branch, but the courts provided little control over police operations. Constables became servers of court orders and sheriffs became jail keepers. The fee-for-service approach of the prior system was replaced by a system of salaried employment, which offered new incentives for crime prevention and order maintenance that had been absent under the earlier system.

The functions of policing expanded considerably in the United States during the nineteenth century. The police by now had become responsible for much more than making arrests: they took in orphans and homeless persons, shot stray dogs, enforced sanitation laws, inspected boilers and fire escapes, and took the annual census (Bayley 1983, 1125; Monkkonen 1992, 554). New York City police officers were assigned the task of cleaning horse droppings from the streets. Many activities associated today with public welfare and public works were once primarily within the domain of municipal policing.

In spite of this broad expansion of responsibilities, some of the core functions that we associate with modern policing remained relegated to the private sector. The Pinkerton National Detective Agency, founded in 1850, served as the primary protector of trains and their passengers in the nineteenth century and maintained the only national crime record system for the seventy five years prior to the creation of the FBI's Uniform Crime Reporting system.[3] A host of other private property protection and investigative agencies emerged not long afterward, including Brink's, Wells Fargo, and Burns. When a criminal investigation was needed, the police department hired private detectives, as did private citizens and other institutions. Bounties remained in widespread use to induce the capture of wanted suspects.

The Reform Era (1890–1930)

The inadequacies of our early municipal police departments had become a political issue toward the end of the nineteenth century. The Progressive movement in particular drew attention to the problems of corruption and incompetence in urban police departments by the 1890s. The Lexow Committee was formed to investigate corruption scandals in the New York City Police Department in 1894; it recommended major reforms of that department. In the following year, Theodore Roosevelt was appointed president of the New York City Police Commission. This provided a foundation from which he was able to establish a reputation as one who acted to clean up politics, starting by replacing the debased system in which police were handmaidens of corrupt ward bosses with a civil service hiring system. He also acted to limit the role of police to that of crime control. The Progressives called for improved screening, so that officers would be better qualified, and for formal training, so that they would be more knowledgeable and competent, and Roosevelt acted to impose those reforms during his three years as de facto New York police commissioner (the post of commissioner was officially created in 1901). At long last, substantive elements of Robert Peel's police reform were adopted in the United States.

These reforms occurred neither overnight nor without frequent setbacks. The Boston Police Department became affiliated with the American Federation of Labor and struck in 1919; rioting and looting followed. Governor Calvin Coolidge mobilized the state militia, fired the police, and then replaced them. The recommendations of the Lexow Committee for police reform were still echoed some thirty years later in recommendations by the Cleveland Crime Commission in 1922, the Missouri Crime Commission in 1926, the Illinois Crime Commission in 1929, and President Herbert Hoover's Wickersham Crime Commission in 1929.

The Emphasis on "Professionalization" (1930–1980)

Many of the Progressive Era reforms served to professionalize law enforcement. Improved screening and training helped to ensure that those sworn to serve the public were fit for the task. Civil service protections helped to reduce pernicious proclivities to control election outcomes and to distance the police somewhat from political influences. Restricting the functions of public policing to issues directly related to crime control helped to provide municipal departments with a sharper sense of focus on a primary mission.

Other developments further contributed to a movement for professionalism in policing. Extraordinary technological advances in transportation, communication, and forensic science during the twentieth century presented seductive opportunities for the police to obtain the symbols of professionalism, if not the substance (P.K. Manning 1977, 130). Two-way radios in speedy patrol vehicles undoubtedly helped to bring about the capture of offenders who would have otherwise committed more crimes, but they also made the police look and feel more competent. Behavioral science was not left out of this technology bandwagon; psychological "instruments" became widely used to make personnel selection and promotion more objective and rigorous, through testing and formal screening procedures. The hard sciences provided the more obvious advantages, offering opportunities for municipal police departments to learn about crimes more systematically and more quickly, to respond more rapidly, and to enhance crime-solving capacities, thus expanding the capacity for overall effectiveness.

The importance of improving effectiveness itself became one of the hallmarks of the professional era of policing.[4] Police leaders began promoting police accomplishments through an expanding and powerful network of media and came to adopt elements of scientific method with the systematic measurement of police effectiveness. This emphasis was not unique to policing, but the police were surely ahead of many other institutions, public and private, in embracing the measurement of performance as a hallmark of excellence, and more specifically as a clear indication that police were professionals.

The application of scientific methodology to policing was the fruit of the work of former bookkeeper August Vollmer, more than anyone else. Vollmer (1971) wrote about and taught the application of scientific method to policing, following the pioneer work of Frederick Taylor on the principles of scientific management, at the nation's first academic program in criminology at the University of California. He had earlier experimented in the use of these principles as marshal of the Berkeley Police Department in the early part of the twentieth century. Most police departments never fully realized Vollmer's prescriptions for scientific approaches to selection and promotion, criminal investigation, and performance evaluation based on crime, arrest, and clearance statistics — because of, in varying degrees, resistance to change, budget constraints, and the unavailability of qualified personnel. But few departments did not travel at least some distance down the trail blazed and promoted by Vollmer.

In 1920 Vollmer proposed the creation of a national bureau of criminal records, to compile data on crimes known to the police. Federal

Bureau of Investigation Director J. Edgar Hoover, with the help of statistician Bruce Smith, developed Vollmer's proposal by deploying a system of Uniform Crime Reporting (UCR) in 1931, which featured standardized definitions of major crime categories and procedures by which police departments began routinely to send counts of reported incidents of crimes and arrests to the FBI.

In taking on the UCR, Hoover attempted to solidify a federal role that had been the rule abroad but without precedent in this country — a central authority of law enforcement, providing a formal (albeit modest) connection among thousands of independent policing agencies throughout the land. The notion that the workload of the police could be measured and analyzed in a manner that would inform policing served also to elevate the status of police, to provide some support to the notion that policing was a profession.

Hoover contributed to another pillar of professionalism, the notion that law enforcement agents are experts, uniquely qualified to solve crimes and catch criminals. His creation of the "Ten Most Wanted" list of criminal suspects, his frequent stimulation of photo-op media accounts of arrests of members of that list, and his prominent display of the FBI's use of forensic technology for solving some of these crimes gave the distinct impression that the organization he had created was without peers when it came to matters of criminal investigation in particular and crime control generally.

Vollmer and Hoover were not alone in their attempts to professionalize the police. Orlando W. Wilson, who served in Vollmer's Berkeley police department, went on to apply Vollmer's ideas of scientific police management as chief of the Fullerton, California, Wichita, Kansas, and Chicago police departments, and to ensure, as dean of the School of Criminology at the University of California, Berkeley, that they were given some academic respectability. In a classic text on police administration, Wilson (1938) expanded on Vollmer's ideas by adding his own ideas about the use of workload statistics to support resource allocation decisions and the use of organization theory to provide a basis for managing police departments.

The quintessential professional era police department, however, was none of those under either Vollmer or Wilson; theirs were works in progress. The apotheosis of the professional model was the Los Angeles Police Department of the 1950s and 1960s, under its chief, William H. Parker. Parker's LAPD emphasized two goals: (1) efficiency in bringing crooks to justice, and (2) a level of integrity that would ensure the complete absence of corruption that had afflicted the LAPD during Prohibition and that continued to plague police departments east of the Rocky Mountains. Parker worked to achieve these goals through by-the-book adherence to rules and stalwart military bearing; the LAPD under Parker prided itself for its "just the facts, ma'am" absence of compassion in bringing crooks to justice. Following J. Edgar Hoover's "Gang Busters" model, Parker was especially effective in gaining the support of the white middle class, largely by showcasing his no-nonsense approach to policing in the hugely popular TV series *Dragnet*, featuring Jack Webb as Sergeant Friday and Chief Parker as principal adviser to the producers of the show.

Vollmer, Hoover, Wilson, Parker, and others who followed their leads transformed the public view of police — and, perhaps more significantly, policing's view of itself — from one grounded in informal custom and ties to local institutions to one based on formal procedure grounded explicitly on utilitarian considerations of justice and distance from the community.[5] As crime rates declined steadily from the inception of the Uniform Crime Reports in 1931 until the early 1960s, these champions of professionalism appeared to have found the magic bullet to crime control.

Police professionals also created a climate in which policing became widely regarded as a legitimate state monopoly. According to one authority, by midcentury, "Policing was now simply assumed to be public . . . Questions about private police and about the relationship between public and private policing simply did not arise" (Shearing 1992, 408).

The Passing-on of Sergeant Friday

The professional era of policing was subjected to its supreme test starting in the mid-1960s — a crime explosion coupled with severe urban unrest. By most accounts it failed that test. A major contributing factor to the eruption of crime was the emergence of the baby boom population into the peak offending ages of fifteen to twenty four. Within the decade starting in 1963, the homicide rate doubled — from 4.5 homicides per 100,000 residents to 8.9 in 1972 — and the robbery and burglary rates more than tripled, with large increases in virtually every other crime category. Meanwhile, riots broke out in New York in 1964, in the Watts area of Los Angeles the following year, in Newark and Detroit in 1967, and in Washington in 1968 following the assassination of Dr. Martin Luther King, Jr.

These developments created demands on municipal police departments that were well beyond the limits of their capacities to respond effectively, especially in the inner cities, where the increases in crime tended to be most extreme. Most crime rates remained at the elevated levels of 1970 throughout the 1970s and 1980s; though homicide rates declined through most of the 1990s, they remained significantly higher than in virtually every other industrialized nation.

Urban riots continued right up through the 1990s, often fueled by overly aggressive, insensitive, and often brutal policing behaviors. The killing of a black motorcyclist by police in Miami in 1979 and the subsequent cover-up by the Metro-Dade, Florida, Police Department's, the Philadelphia police bombing of the MOVE headquarters in 1985, and the Los Angeles police beating of Rodney King in 1991 are three of the more conspicuous examples (Skolnick and Fyfe 1993). Police brutality was, of course, not unique to the professional era of policing; it was perhaps more common in earlier times. But it was met with a public reaction that had been unknown even as recently as the 1950s. It was becoming increasingly clear that a style of policing that had been popular especially among white middle-class Americans and among much of the police force was one that was capable of brutalizing large segments of the population. Even in the absence of brutality, professional policing was viewed by large segments of the minority community as cold and cruel.

Professionalism did not invent brutality, but it did foster a vast separation between the police and the community. The notion that police were the experts contributed to police arrogance and a sense among the police that members of the community were inferior. Effective use of technology and emphasis on efficiency need not interfere with a healthy relationship between the police and the public, but the leaders of the professional era managed to replace a friendly service attitude with a cool, detached one and thus to severely damage that relationship. Police in many jurisdictions further alienated the public by spending less and less time on the street.[6] There is nothing inherently wrong, and much right, about the idea of the police working to achieve the status of professional, but the brand of professionalism preached by the most prominent spokespersons for the professional movement and practiced by their minions clearly contradicted the most fundamental we-the-people aspects of democracy (Toch 1997). The bubble had burst. The police had succeeded in restricting their mission to crime control, only to discover that their ability to control crime was severely limited.

Community Policing

By the mid-1980s, it was clear that a different approach to policing was needed. Not only was the professional model shown to be ill suited for the areas where crime was most serious, but research was revealing that it was ill suited for other areas as well:

1. In 1973, Police Foundation researchers reported finding that saturating areas in Kansas City with random patrol squad cars had no deterrent effect whatever on the amount of crime in the area (Kelling et al. 1974).
2. In 1982, researchers working in Flint, Michigan, reported finding that officers patrolling on foot had a much higher rate of nonconfrontational contact with citizens, and a much lower rate of confrontational contact, than motorized patrol officers; also, both calls for service and crime declined in areas where there were foot patrols (Trojanowicz et al. 1982).
3. In 1985, Police Foundation researchers working with the Houston and Newark police departments reported finding that a variety of interventions in those two cities that brought the police closer to the community — including miniprecincts, foot patrols, and door-to-door police outreach contacts — tended to reduced fear, increase satisfaction with police service, and increase the perceived quality of life (Pate et al. 1985).

The general idea for a new style of policing was to return to much of what was good about an earlier style of policing. This meant getting closer to the community, not only to improve relations between the police and community — a worthy end in itself — but also to become more familiar with the problems that were unique to specific areas and to develop contacts that would help the police, in *partnership* with the public, to both prevent and solve crimes.[7]

It meant also an expanded view of what policing was about — not just law enforcement but crime prevention and fear reduction. A few police chiefs, such as Lee Brown, chief of the Houston Police Department in the mid-1980s and then commissioner of the New York Police Department in the early 1990s, took it a step further: the police should aim for no less than working to improve the quality of life in the community so that people could once again enjoy and feel safe in public parks and facilities and walk down the street without being subjected to the signs of crime — graffiti, abandoned vehicles, and broken windows (Brown 1989; Wilson and Kelling 1982).

A host of other characteristics have come to be associated with community policing: more officer autonomy and less centralized organizational hierarchy; greater reliance on the informal exercise of discretion and less on formal rules and regulations; and a shift from a mode of random patrol and rapid response to calls for service from a central precinct station to one involving greater use of foot and bicycle patrols and miniprecincts. Above all, the community policing movement amounts to a return to fundamental democratic principles of governance: that the police *serve* the public, that they are *accountable* to the public, and that the public has a *voice* in determining how the police will serve them.

The community policing movement has been met with considerable resistance from some quarters, much of it based on legitimate concerns. First, the concept has a fad quality; it is easily trivialized. Many, perhaps most, police departments have embraced the form and rhetoric of community policing and largely ignored its substance. Second, though corruption has not yet revealed itself to be a problem unique to community policing, the risk that corruptible police who are closer to the public will succumb to corruption pressures, especially in cities with traditions of corruption, cannot be ignored. Third, high-crime areas are often devoid of the social organization that we generally associate with definitions of "community." Field experiments have revealed that poor inner-city areas tend not to show the gains found in other areas after community policing interventions are applied — improved satisfaction with police service, reduced fear of crime, improvements in perceived quality of life (Skogan 1990, 166–67). Fourth, for all the rhetoric about the potential crime-reducing ability of strengthened police-public partnership, there is little evidence that community policing interventions have had a systematic effect on crime rates.

In short, community policing offers the potential to improve the delivery of service by the police. It does not promise that they will be able to prevent or respond effectively to every sort of future problem of crime and disorder. It does present opportunities to make policing more nearly consistent with fundamental principles of democracy: public service, accountability, and voice. It is an approach to policing that could be effectively used primarily by the police and by private security agents as well.

The Resurgence of Private Protection

The professional era of policing is being superseded by community policing largely because it has presented to the public the view that the police, not the public, are the primary line of defense against crime. This illusion has had regrettable consequences: both the police and the public were all too willing to accept the idea that the public were primarily pawns in the matter. The heroic images portrayed by the FBI's "Gang Busters" and by *Dragnet's* Sergeant Friday were elixirs for a public fearful of crime, a public eager to relieve itself of responsibility for maintaining order and enforcing informal rules of behavior through age-old forces for policing lapses in social conformity: consistent use of parental discipline, inducements toward mannerly behavior, use of shame, and so on.[8]

As the police have demonstrated that their powers in dealing with crime and threats of terrorism since the 1960s have in fact been quite limited and as public funds have become increasingly scarce, reliance on these age-old social inducements has not reemerged in a systematic fashion. Other, more tangible private-sector responses have materialized in their place. Private expenditures for security equipment, personnel, and services have soared — in office buildings, subways and other public transportation systems, shopping centers and warehouses, universities and schools, hospitals, and large apartment complexes and condominiums. Passenger and baggage screening is routinely handled today at airports by private security firms under contract with the airlines, and local police are called in for emergencies ("Policing for Profit" 1997; Newman 1997; Stewart 1985). The proportion of homes with alarm systems increased from 1 percent in 1975 to 10 percent in 1985 (Gest 1985), with no signs that the trend has abated in the years since.

Privatization has occurred also in the areas of investigative services, perimeter safeguards, surveillance systems, risk management, and armed courier and armored car services (Becker, 1995; "Policing for Profit" 1997). Private investigation alone now encompasses services that range from the investigation of disability claims and marital infidelity and the delivery of legal papers (process serving) to criminal investigations aimed at undermining the prosecutor's evidence and solving sophisticated computer crimes.

The public has come to recognize that their municipal police departments have limited capacities, and they have taken matters into their own hands. They have hired private agents for specific security services, and do other services themselves: citizen foot patrols and block watches, escort services for senior citizens and university women, citizen-band radio automobile patrols, and radio-alert networks for taxis, buses, and commercial vehicles. Laws permitting private citizens to carry concealed weapons became increasingly popular in the 1990s. The police no longer monopolize public safety. Additional privatization has occurred as police departments have contracted out to private agencies for a variety of services: court security, prisoner custody, computer and communications system maintenance, training, laboratory services, radio dispatching, video surveillance, and traffic and parking control.[9]

Some communities, aware of the inefficiencies in providing conventional police services, have bypassed their police departments altogether and contracted out portions of public protective services to private agencies. Los Angeles County awarded some thirty-six contracts for guard services in the early 1980s at an estimated 74 percent of the cost of the county policing alternative (Savas 1982, 183).[10] Other municipalities have gone even further, experimenting with all-private police forces, and have found them to have delivered services at lower costs with no decline in quality of service.[11]

Viewed historically, the shift has been sudden. It took centuries for public policing to establish dominance over paid private security agents and less than two decades for the trend to reverse itself. The number of private security employees and expenditures for private security, which had paled against those for the police in the early 1960s, had matched the corresponding numbers for public police by about 1975, had doubled it by 1985, and had surpassed the public counterpart by a factor of perhaps three by 1990 (Shearing and Stenning 1981, 203; Cunningham and Taylor 1985, 112). While most police departments have grown modestly since 1975, the private security industry has mushroomed.

These developments have not been unique to the United States. A 1988 survey in the United Kingdom found 239 patrols operated by private firms on behalf of local authorities (*Police Review* 1989). Britain and Canada had twice as many private security agents as public police by 1990 (Fielding 1991; Toronto Police Department 1990). Similar trends have been reported in Australia, Switzerland, Bavaria, and elsewhere (Rau 1989; Elliott 1991).

Nor are they unique to policing. Private correctional institutions constituted only 19 percent of all juvenile correctional facilities in the United States in 1950; they grew to 41 percent of all such institutions by 1989.[13] During the same period the number of inmates held in private centers grew from zero to 7 percent of the total federal prisoner population (Bronick 1989). Privatization has occurred as well in the delivery of ambulance service, fire protection, libraries, sewerage, trash collection, street maintenance, legal services for indigent defendants, and alternatives to adjudication, such as mediation and diversion programs. Lopez de Silanes, Shleifer, and Vishny (1995) have estimated from recent censuses of governments that the fraction of twelve such services contracted out by 3,043 U.S. counties increased from 24 percent to 34 percent from 1987 to 1992.

Lopez de Silanes, Shleifer, and Vishny go on to investigate the correlates with the fraction of government services contracted out. They find that the counties with the largest fractions of services contracted out tend to be those with laws that discourage political patronage (e.g., laws requiring merit systems for hiring and laws setting local purchasing standards for county spending), laws that restrict unionization of and strikes by public employees, laws that constrain the government budgeting process (e.g., debt limits, restrictions on short-term borrowing), and counties that give larger percentages of votes for Republican governors. Political ideology of the voters appears to have been a fairly small determinant of the movement toward privatization.[14]

Although comparisons in effectiveness have been made between public and private counterparts providing similar services, global comparisons cannot be made. The varieties of private security forces are so vast — as are public police agencies — that it is virtually impossible to make meaningful generalizations about the relative superiority, effectiveness, or costs of either broad sector. They range from well-trained and well-paid agents, often current or former sworn officers who operate in coordination with municipal police departments, to plant guards whose job is simply to call the police when they observe suspicious activities, to vigilante groups and ganglike organizations that often compete with local police for the control of neighborhoods.[15] Even the least formally organized persons operating in a private security capacity have the authority to arrest that is granted to ordinary citizens, although the laws governing that authority are somewhat murky.[16]

Did the arrogance associated with the professional era of policing that has induced the promotion of a kinder and gentler style of policing contribute as well to the growth of the private security industry? Perhaps, but the industry would certainly have grown anyway. There is no clear indication that the transition to community policing has slowed that growth appreciably; the hiring of security personnel that accompanied the rapid development of shopping malls in the 1980s was not a direct product of police arrogance. Regardless of whether police arrogance played a major or minor role in stimulating the private security business, however, community policing's bridge-building motif is by all appearances more hospitable to private security than the ivory tower approach of professionalism (Walsh and Donovan 1989).

Privatization of protective services is, in any case, not new. As I have noted above, protection from crime and disorder was once exclusively a private matter; the recent trend toward privatization follows centuries of what might be referred to as the "publicization" of police services.

The recent movement toward the privatization of policing is perhaps best explained by its parallel to a general decline in the willingness of voters to incur higher taxes and support government expansion, and a specific decline in their willingness to see their tax dollars leave their communities.

Such sentiments are not unique to conservative Americans. According to the prolific mainstream management scholar Peter Drucker (1988, 30), "Government has become too big, too complex, too remote for each citizen actively to participate in it . . . we no longer believe, as did the 'liberals' and 'progressives' these past hundred years, that community tasks can — nay, should — be left to government." Such sentiments have been voiced as well by Vice President Al Gore, who, in heading the National Performance Review, asks how Americans can be expected to trust and respect government when, on average, they believe it wastes forty-eight cents of every tax dollar it collects (Gore 1993, 1). Gore (1993, 1995) envisions a government that will come to rely increasingly on privatization, point-of-service vouchers, inter- and intra-agency competition, and the creation of performance-based organizations that can be managed like private corporations.[17]

The History of Public and Private Policing: Recapitulation

What significant patterns are revealed from this brief account of the history of public and private policing? One is that sweeping changes in policing trends have emerged, typically as manifestations of broader societal movements. The reform era of policing grew out of the larger reform era that transformed the corrupt political machines of the nineteenth century into institutions that were held more widely accountable. Police professionalism reflected in part a desire of police to take advantage of the technological advances that were transforming the society at large. The community policing movement of the 1980s was largely an outgrowth of trends in consumerism, excellence in service delivery, and "empowerment" crusades of the times.

In a similar manner, the fairly recent twenty-year trend back to privatization in policing, after nearly two centuries of growth in public police departments, corresponds with a larger dissatisfaction with government services and rising taxes. Elsewhere in the criminal justice system, especially in the corrections area, privatization has taken shape, not without the controversy that has accompanied the privatization of policing services. Fire and ambulance services have been privatized in many communities, and people are turning increasingly to alternatives to public school systems — private schools, with and without public subsidy in the form of vouchers, and home schooling. At the federal level, serious consideration is being given to the privatization of the Social Security system (Dentzer 1996), at least in part, as well as to privatization of the mail delivery and air traffic control systems, public housing, and government printing operations (Hage et al. 1995).[18]

The second major pattern is this: significant reforms in the delivery of public policing services have typically followed failure of the prevailing system to deal effectively with newly emerging threats. The creation of the London MPD and the use of uniformed officers in major U.S. cities in the early and mid-nineteenth century were responses to breakdowns in order associated with the Industrial Revolution's flood of immigrants to urban centers in search of jobs. The reform era of policing was largely a response to public disgust with rampant police corruption. The community policing era emerged as central elements of "police professionalism" revealed themselves to be not only ineffective but often counterproductive, stimulants of frustration and anger in minority communities. August Vollmer and Orlando Wilson's concepts of professionalism in policing surely were not designed to promote arrogance, insensitivity, and brutality, yet professionalism nonetheless became a cloak within which those evils came to masquerade. Proponents of community policing would certainly do well to ensure that their good intentions are not similarly corrupted.

The third major pattern has to do with the pervasiveness of private solutions to problems of crime and disorder. In the absence of a corps of sworn officers, or when the government fails to provide effective protection, private protective services tend to fill the void.[19] The central functions of policing — preserving domestic peace and order, preventing and responding to crimes — have always been conducted first, foremost, and predominantly by private means. Even during periods in which the number of sworn police officers exceeded the number of paid security personnel, the vast majority of activities and expenditures associated with crime have been private. Most crimes still are not reported to the police; in 1994 only 41.6 percent of violent crimes and 32.6 percent of personal thefts were reported to the police (Perkins and Klaus 1996).

The exception is in the domain of the most serious crimes: the highest concentrations of sworn police officers relative to private protective service personnel have tended to be in the activity of responding to homicides, robberies, and other serious felonies. More commonplace demands for protection against crime, and crime prevention in particular, have always relied more heavily on private solutions. Even in the business of responding to serious crimes, however, public services have often faltered in the presence of overwhelming obstacles, leaving no choice but for citizens to fend for themselves. The failure of the Los Angeles Police Department to deal effectively with the riots in Los Angeles following a Simi Valley jury's acquittal of police officers charged with beating Rodney King is a prominent example. The anarchic private responses that emerge under such extraordinary circumstances are often at sharp odds with conventional notions of justice, not unlike the gunslinging scenarios that characterized the fabled Old West frontier of the United States during the nineteenth century.

❏ PRIVATIZATION AND PUBLICIZATION: A PRESCRIPTIVE ASSESSMENT

The developments described above unfolded with varying degrees of deliberation as to the appropriate role of police and the degrees to which each aspect of policing should be provided publicly or privately. The absence of deliberation has had its consequences; the most serious problems in policing appear to have occurred when police departments operate exclusively in a reactive mode rather than one that anticipates and heads off significant problems before they overwhelm preexisting police capacities.

A more contemplative approach would begin by identifying each aspect of policing that might be delivered publicly or privately and asking how public and private approaches to the delivery of each aspect can be expected to affect each of the following: (1) the overall quality and quantity of services delivered, (2) the costs of delivery, (3) the distribution of services to high- and low-income citizens, and (4) the ability of citizens to choose among alternative service delivery strategies. I consider such a framework below, after first summarizing the primary strengths and weaknesses of private security alternatives to public policing.

The Strengths and Weaknesses of Privatization

Specific advantages presented by the private security alternative to a force of public officers include the following, the first four of which are common to private sector goods and services generally:

1. The buyer of an agency's services can replace the entire agency when it fails to deliver desired levels of service quality.
2. Management can more easily dismiss individual personnel who fail to conform to agency standards KlocKars 1985, pp. 40–62.
3. Governmental accounting procedures are biased against efficient resource allocation.[21]

4. Private organizations have strong incentives to respond to specific and diverse user needs, suggestions, and complaints, and can often do so more quickly, without the requirement for such communications to wend their way through cumbersome municipal bureaucracies.[22]

5. Private security agencies tend to be more receptive to innovation and risk than do municipal police departments (Sparrow et al. 1990, 202–8).

6. Private agents have the authority to stop and challenge any person, without probable cause, for trespassing in a designated private area,[23] and they can make arrests without having to give *Miranda* warnings to arrestees (Walsh and Donovan 1989, 195; Jacobs 1983, 1141).

7. Municipal police departments may be able to reduce patrols in areas covered privately, thus freeing up resources for other public needs (Jacobs 1983, 1140).

8. The delivery of police services and specific police functions (such as vehicle towing and laboratory analysis of forensic evidence), like the production of other services and goods, are subject to economies of scale — an approximate size that minimizes costs per unit of service delivered — that private organizations are more likely forces to achieve than public (Poole 1978, 28).

These advantages suggest that private security agents can serve to complement sworn police officers, filling gaps in public service. A central aspect of this complementarity is that the police are saddled with an open-ended and hence more daunting task than are security guards: protecting public places rather than private property (Sherman 1995, 339). The private security industry may thus be able to serve citizens both by serving specific private needs at the margins where public streets and private property converge and by providing a counterweight to public policing authorities, reducing monopoly powers and political influences that have been known to breed inefficiency and even mean-spirited service.[25]

Private security agents are not generally bound by the same set of constraints that are imposed on sworn police officers. They enjoy the powers to arrest, to search for and seize evidence, and to file criminal charges in court, but they are not held to due process requirements routinely followed by the police, such as those specified in *Mapp v. Ohio*.[26] This latitude offers to private agents a degree of immunity from criminal or civil liability charges arising from false arrests that sworn officers must often face.[27] Unlike sworn officers, who are bound to file criminal charges when probable cause exists, private security personnel have discretion to prosecute offenders under either civil (advantageous to stores in cases involving affluent shoplifters) or criminal statutes (generally used for poor offenders), thus raising questions about equal protection and due process (Davis et al. 1991).

Affluent voters have been willing to tax themselves for police services in their communities at prevailing margins and to augment those funds with private security expenditures targeted on specific needs, but many have been less than thrilled to see their tax dollars leave their immediate communities to go elsewhere within the jurisdiction. Obviously, a private citizen has substantially more control over funds spent on private protection services than over funds aimed at public police that must traverse convoluted governmental processes, and it should not be surprising that they would vote accordingly. A common self-interested attitude seems to go along the following line: "I'm tired of trying endlessly to bail out the inner cities with my tax dollars; let them take care of themselves for a change. I can keep pretty much to my neighborhood and be responsible for my own protection, public and private." As good jobs have left urban centers over the past twenty years, it has become all too easy for upper- and middle-class voters to separate themselves from the problem of inner-city crime (W. J. Wilson 1987). Federal and state expenditures on policing are more easily distributable to inner cities than are local expenditures, but political pressures often intervene to thwart even those redistributions.

Thus one of the acute problems of privatization has been to allow areas most in need of protective services to go without them, which only adds to the vulnerability of the residents of those neighborhoods to crime and disorder. The Metropolitan Police Department of Washington, D.C. has come under extreme financial stress in the late 1990s while neighborhoods in many of the District of Columbia's affluent northwest area can protect themselves privately and as the suburbs surrounding the nation's capital experience low crime rates and well-financed police departments. Police departments operating within the metropolitan areas of New Orleans, Detroit, Richmond, Virginia and other places with extremes of inner-city crime in the general vicinity of wealthy suburbs have come to experience similar disparities in protection.

This is by no means the only problem associated with the privatization of policing. Another is that a private corporation and its employees can be difficult to supervise, especially when the contracts are awarded to different companies periodically. This can become a noxious matter when the private agents have access to sensitive information. Though public officials occasionally violate privacy, as in the 1996 case of the White House rifling through over four hundred FBI security files of political opponents without legitimate justification (Gergen 1996), the potential for such violations could be greater when private agencies have access to such information. Government employees can be held to a higher standard. They are accountable not only to the highest level of political authority, but to the public, in ways that private individuals are not (*Washington Post* 1996).

Another potential problem with privatization derives from one of the most basic aspects of our criminal justice system: the adversarial system of legal procedure reduces the role of vengeance by interposing the state in the place of the victim as the offender's legal opponent. This is viewed by many as a fundamental weakness of our system of justice, one that depersonalizes the process and moves those most directly harmed by crime off into a role of prosecution resource, imposing an excessive burden of uncompensated crime and justice costs on the victims. The police have long been known to view our legal system with suspicion and hostility (Skolnick 1994, 181–9: 213–20),[28] and this feature of our system surely contributes to the breach between the police and legal cultures. Several scholars have noted that this cultural divergence lies beneath episodes of police brutality delivered as "curbside justice," an act of using dirty means to achieve what some individuals view as worthy ends (Klockars 1995, 330–40; Skolnick and Fyfe 1993, 106–12).

This has been a problem primarily with sworn police officers rather than private security agents, and the privatization of policing does not alter this basic constitutional principle of our justice system. Yet the extralegal retributive behaviors that have become a too-familiar feature of our policing culture could conceivably become more widespread under further privatization. The police officer is insulated from the victim through several layers of mid- and upper-level police management and a mayor's office; in a properly functioning department, abuses in the use of force may result in job loss and difficulty of finding another job in policing. The security agent working directly for a client victim, on the other hand, may be more inclined to do the client's bidding for brutal tough justice, especially when his job security may be strengthened by the activity.[29] Bar bouncers and bodyguards are rarely known for their reputations as civil libertarians, and an expansion of these uncontrolled and often overly aggressive branches of the private security industry would not bode well for the goal of a more civil society.

Perhaps the most difficult problem of private security personnel is that the potential for incompetence and misbehavior is enormous. The screening for many private hirings is often lax and the training nil. Poor screening has been known to result in the hiring of private security personnel with criminal records.[30] Security guards may receive guns without having re-

ceived adequate instruction on their usage.[31] They may receive uniforms
and be assigned beats to patrol when they are unprepared for even routine
situations.[32] And poorly managed agencies and unscrupulous operators
have been known to go bankrupt or otherwise fail to honor contractual
assurances that their services and products — alarm systems, locking
devices, and so on — are up to par (Stewart 1985, 762).

The fundamental issue is that of *legitimacy*. Police officers take an oath
of office in which they swear to serve the public at large; they are neither
narrowly nor tentatively employed. Though some officers clearly do not
follow the oath as earnestly as others, most are likely to take it seriously as
a commitment to public service over self-interested behavior.[33] Few private
security agents are bound by solemn vows to serve the public.[34] Such a
commitment not only may serve the public more effectively, but may
produce the side benefit of contributing to the building of character — a
trait that has, regrettably, lost currency in contemporary matters[35] — perhaps
even inducing citizens to participate more in the democratic process.

Ebbs and Flows in Privatization and the Privatization Debate

One characteristic of the privatization debate, as with virtually all
debates, is a tendency for proponents on one side or the other to romanticize
the strengths of its favored side and denigrate the weaknesses of the other.
Proponents of privatization tend to overlook the problems of disparity in the
quality and quantity of services delivered to high-crime, poor inner-city
neighborhoods on the one hand and to relatively peaceful, affluent suburbs
on the other, as well as the other problems noted above. Here is one example
of some thinly veiled propaganda for the privatization movement:

> (T)he business of the private security sector is not only to sell safety and
> security but to educate people in the many ways they can protect themselves.
> This important service makes private security a natural ally of the police and
> formidable foe of the criminal. Together we can fashion a program which will
> foster public understanding and enlist public assistance in combating crime.
> Both police and private security stand to gain, but more importantly, the
> public stands to gain the most: a safe and tranquil community in which to
> live and work. (Shook 1997, 7–10).[36]

Others are inclined to see considerable evil and little good in privatization. Clifford Shearing, for example, characterizing privatization as

"emerging corporate feudalism" (1992, 423), criticizes Cunningham et al. for their laissez-faire "reform agenda": (T)he acceptance and promotion of corporate guarantors of order, with their feudal resonances of relatively autonomous nonstate corporate entities, creates a tension within the laissez-faire framework that gestures toward a more fractured conception of policing that denies the state its privileged position" (p. 421).[37] When one's overarching concern is a belief in the inherent privileged position of the state (or the private sector) — when one sees the state (or the corporation) as something other than a servant of the people — discussion of the shortcomings of privatization (or publicization) tends to be more thorough than that of the problems associated with state-run monopolies (or market economies).

Some have noted that a particular danger associated with the growth of the private security industry is that police agencies will lose public support and authority when the public perceives that their services are inferior to those of the private alternative.[38] This notion may overlook a more basic relationship between the growth of the private security industry and the perceived quality of public police service — namely, that the former is more likely the *result* of the latter rather than the cause. Though the many problems of privatization must not be overlooked, the existence of a private security alternative may nonetheless be a positive influence, one that can complement the police and serve to induce police departments to improve the quality of their services.

More fundamentally, we have witnessed a swing from complete privatization and its shortcomings to an era of virtual public monopoly of security services by 1960, and now the pendulum swings back toward privatization. Has the pendulum swung too far in the direction of privatization? What should be the basis for making such an assessment? By 1994, about four dollars were consumed in the private sector of the U.S. economy for every dollar consumed in the public sector;[39] meanwhile, roughly two dollars were spent for private security resources for every dollar spent on public policing. Do these numbers correspond to ones we might derive from a thoughtful prescriptive calculus? Can we envision a more stable and coherent system, one that doesn't swing from one extreme to the other? Let us explore a general framework for addressing these issues.

Public and Private Goods

It will be essential to consider separately each major aspect of policing that may be delivered privately or publicly, but it will be useful first to think about a context within which each of those aspects can be weighed. Economic theory provides the standard utilitarian context, one that begins by making a basic distinction between public and private goods. A *public good* (or service) is one for which the benefits are nonexcludable and indivisible; they accrue to society at large rather than to specific individuals who may wish to pay for the good.[40] To the extent that police deter crimes, all citizens will benefit. Other examples include the court and correctional systems, national defense, and freeway construction. The level and quality of such goods and services are determined through political processes. A *private good* is one for which the benefits accrue only to those who pay for the good. Examples include automobile ownership and the viewing of motion pictures. The level and quality of such goods and services are determined through the market economy.

Domestic security falls in both camps — it confers both private and public benefits on individuals. People who pay for private security generally experience benefits that justify the costs. Improved locks and alarm systems confer benefits directly on those who pay for them. The community as a whole, on the other hand, generally experiences benefits from having a safer environment to a degree that justifies the public expenditures for police departments. Police officers patrolling parks, streets, and other public places confer benefits on all who may wish to frequent them. Dependence on private funding for the policing of such places can, however, present a *free-rider* problem: policing public areas through reliance on private support will be underfunded to the extent that some individuals renege on their obligation and let others pay for the service. Private citizens can overcome free-rider problems privately by setting up homeowner organizations or similar quasi-public institutions with voting and dues-paying arrangements to select and acquire specific levels and types of security resources. Thus the free-rider problem does not require that the government must provide the public good, only that it or a quasi-public counterpart serve as collection agent for its provision.

These constructs can help to inform the debate on the privatization of policing. They lend coherence to the process of organizing and assessing key elements of both privatization and policing. The market economy is often criticized for its failure to deal with inequitable distributions of goods and services and for the occurrence of external diseconomies — as prevails in privatization when, for example, one citizen's quality of life is diminished by the intrusive behavior of a private detective, by the accidental discharge of a weapon obtained for protective purposes,[41] or by the existence of a neighbor's excessively barking watchdog.[42] The public sector is often criticized for inefficiencies that result from public agents who are shielded from competitive inducements to maintain high levels of service quality and quantity.[43]

The partitioning of public and private policing services can thus be understood as the result of a loose interplay of political and private decision processes. Private security expenditures are largely the product of a combination of perceived inadequacies in public protection and the ability of people to purchase protective goods and services in the private sector. The mix of public and private resources in any neighborhood will be determined by the level and mix of crime, the quality and quantity of public policing service, and the wealth and political power of the people in the neighborhood. Wealthy communities are generally willing and able to tax themselves more for public police *and* to purchase more private protection as well. It is no coincidence that wealthy communities tend to experience lower rates of burglary, larceny, and robbery despite a greater abundance of potential loot.[44]

Pertinent Aspects of Policing

What primary aspects of policing can be identified to permit a comprehensive assessment of the ability of public and private alternatives to contribute to the key aspects of police performance: effectiveness, cost, equity, and choice? Egon Bittner (1980) has identified three primary domains of policing: (1) criminal law enforcement, (2) regulatory control, and (3) peacekeeping. The *law enforcement* domain includes both responses to calls for service and discretionary enforcement activities associated with the control of crimes of consent: prostitution, gambling, and drugs. It also includes undercover operations to avert violent street crimes and fencing of stolen property. The *regulatory control* domain includes traffic management and the control of specific licensed activities, such as vendor licenses, permits to carry firearms, taxicab licenses, and hotel registration. The *peacekeeping* domain includes order maintenance activities such as crowd control, handling complaints against disorderly neighbors, dealing with mentally ill and suicidal individuals, control of youthful disorders and gang activities, and coordination with public works agencies to repair street surfaces and faulty lighting and to remove abandoned vehicles. It includes as well responding to emergencies and disasters. Few of the peacekeeping functions are in response to crimes, but most do involve an element of latent conflict and the prospect of a criminal offense, particularly in urban areas (N. Fyfe 1995; Wilson and Kelling 1982).

One can further distinguish operational and support activities of police departments as aspects suitable for privatization. The three domains identified above by Bittner represent *operational activities*. Typical police department *support activities* include human resource management, call-taking and dispatch operations, vehicle maintenance, forensic evidence analysis, information systems management, research and strategic planning, and financial management.

Walsh and Donovan offer yet another categorization of policing tasks that have been performed by a private security agency serving a Brooklyn high-rise apartment complex: (1) law enforcement activities, mostly responding to calls involving complaints (43 percent of all tasks); (2) miscellaneous services to residents, such as assisting elderly persons with packages, providing escorts during evening hours, and giving street directions (20 percent); (3) crime prevention activities, such as checking parking garages, stairwells, and other public areas for suspicious persons, events and vehicles (17 percent); (4) service for management (10 percent); and (5) administrative duties (10 percent) (1989, 191). These activities are not typical of ones engaged in by private security agencies. They resemble more closely the sorts of activities that are commonly performed by community-oriented patrol officers in municipal police departments.

Table 1.1 provides a worksheet for organizing this information in terms of the extent to which specific public and private alternatives contribute to the goals of policing for each type of service provided. I do not fill out the matrix here because the responses vary from community to community, from one police department to another, and among a virtually limitless array of private sector alternatives for dealing with a particular security service. It is provided primarily as a framework for coherent analysis.

Even without data for a particular community, perusal of the matrix permits some preliminary observations. It should be apparent, for example, that for the activities for which the most is at stake — issues that present immediate threats to life and limb — effectiveness and equity ought to be the most critical criteria for assessing performance. For such activities, carefully screened and well-trained individuals are essential, people who know what to do in a variety of routine yet serious situations and who can be trusted to exercise discretion wisely for situations that fall outside the routine. Sworn police officers are generally most appropriate for such circumstances, despite the higher costs that typically prevail.

Regulatory functions would seem also to call primarily for sworn officers. These functions are more susceptible to danger of corruption, and success in the careers of sworn officers is more critically tied to absence of

TABLE 1.1 Matrix for Assessing Public and Private Alternatives for Each Goal of Policing by Aspect of Policing

Aspect of Policing	Effectiveness	Cost	Equity	Choice
Law enforcement				
Responding to telephone calls for service				
Responding to automatic burglar alarm calls				
Enforcing vice laws				
Engaging in undercover operations				
Crimes of violence				
Fencing of stolen goods				
Regulatory control				
Traffic management				
Firearm permits				
Vendor, taxi licenses				
Hotel, restaurant control				
Peacekeeping functions				
Crowd control				
Handling noise complaints				
Managing special events				
Handling mentally ill, suicidal individuals				
Handling disorderly juveniles				
Escorting Prisoners				
Responding to emergency, disaster				
Coordination with public works for repairs, removals				
Miscellaneous crime prevention activities				
Target hardening: surveillance systems, alarms				
Community service				
Giving directions				
Miscellaneous bridge-building, support activities				
Support activities				
Human resource management				
Call taking, dispatch				
Forensic evidence analysis				
Vehicle maintenance				
Information systems management				
Research, strategic planning				
Financial management				

wrongdoing than is the case with privately hired employees, who may be more inclined to move from one job to another. Though corruption is certainly not unknown to sworn officers in many police departments, most citizens would probably prefer police officers over contract employees for regulating activities that affect public safety and order.

Enforcement of vice laws, similarly, is inherently and primarily a matter for the police, since these are laws against acts that have no immediate victims. Though trafficking in illegal goods and services often imposes substantial costs on the neighborhoods in which it occurs, the absence of a victim who might ordinarily purchase protection against a crime of violence or immediate property loss places the primary burden of enforcement of vice laws and investigation of vice crimes squarely on sworn police officers. The indirect costs to affected neighborhoods may, of course, be dealt with through private means.

On the other hand, "target hardening" (e.g., the installation and maintenance of surveillance and alarm systems), responding to burglar alarms, and police support activities are ones that would seem to lend themselves to a greater extent to service from private sector employees. Private police protect individuals and private property, while sworn officers police public places. Target hardening is already a predominantly private matter, and police departments are seeking and finding ways of reducing responses to false alarms. Since 1960, they have also been moving generally in the direction of civilianization of many of the support functions listed in Table 1 to reduce costs and improve effectiveness by hiring specialists to perform such activities as information systems management and administration of finance and accounting functions.

The very existence of questions about when private policing solutions may be superior to public solutions suggests that in such ambiguous circumstances *both* solutions may be in order, with the respective roles to be worked out as unique local conditions dictate. Here are some examples of ambiguous circumstances: enforcement of parking codes, animal control, security for special events, funeral escorts, prisoner escorts, public housing security, and small town policing. The best mix of public and private solutions in these domains is bound to vary from community to community, depending on existing police workloads, the quality of local government, the extent of income inequality, and other factors.[45]

In any case, a given community does not have to continue providing for its security needs just as it has historically up to the present. By considering each aspect of its security needs and asking how the various public and private alternatives support each of the fundamental goals of security — effectiveness, cost, equity, and choice — citizens may find ample opportunities to improve the delivery of those services.

Private Security Systems and the Poor

One issue that warrants special consideration is the handling of residential and commercial security systems. The benefits of burglar alarm systems are both direct and indirect, as are the costs. The direct benefit is reduced burglaries and other crimes that often accompany burglary, either through the deterrent value of discouraging burglaries or through the enhanced ability to catch crimes in progress. Indirect benefits include peace of mind; avoidance of the need to remain on the premises, away from other activities, in order to protect one's property; and any external benefits to neighbors associated with the perception that buildings in the area are protected.[46] The direct costs consist of the initial outlays for installation and the utility charges for maintenance. Indirect costs include the costs of false alarms imposed on the police — a cost that is shared by citizens who do not have the systems[47] — and a decline in the quality of life associated with signs that perpetually remind us of a need to protect ourselves, even when the dangers may be modest.[48] Some have argued that these security systems may be inferior to architectural designs and urban configurations that discourage crime without such costs (Brantingham and Brantingham 1990; Clarke 1992; Flusty 1994).

Residential surveys and ethnographic studies have demonstrated that private alarm systems can be an effective deterrent,[49] but what about a downside of their use beyond cost: their limited availability to the poor, who are typically at greatest risk of victimization and least able to afford such resources? Privatization has been less controversial in the area of prevention than in the control of crime, but as police have come to take on additional responsibility for prevention, it seems in order to consider what should be done in areas where private spending on alarm systems and other forms of crime detection and prevention has been limited by a dearth of resources. Simon Hakim and his colleagues (1996) have devised one creative solution: the costs of false alarms and problems associated with inaccessibility of the systems to the poor can be handled simultaneously by imposing a system of fines for repeat false alarms, in amounts no less than an approximation of the average cost of each such call,[50] and using the resulting revenues to subsidize the installation of alarms and other prevention systems for the poor. An alternative solution would be for private security agents rather than sworn police officers to respond to all automatic alarm calls so that the consumers of those services bear the costs, and to solve the problem of inequitable distribution of home protection by providing families who cannot afford alarm systems with the means to pay for them, much as food stamps are currently provided to assist poor families to help them pay for basic necessities. These subsidies can simultaneously support the effectiveness, cost, equity, and choice goals.

One might be tempted to argue that opportunities to conserve scarce police resources through privatization are greatest in the domain of protecting commercial establishments. Businesses are, after all, better able to cover the costs of protection than are poor residents of a community. This argument, however, may apply more appropriately to wealthy than to poor neighborhoods. It overlooks the typical response of businesses everywhere to crime and its costs. It is well known that high crime rates in many neighborhoods have induced higher prices, lower-quality goods and services, and eventually, the emigration of commercial institutions out of those places (W. J. Wilson 1987). The allocation of sworn police officers to poor neighborhoods, supported by general public revenues, should not be restricted to public streets and residential areas. At current margins, the returns to public safety and public welfare may actually be higher for additional allocations of sworn officers to protect commercial establishments in poor neighborhoods than for alternative allocations in those areas.

Legitimacy

If any single concern is paramount, it is that of *legitimacy*. The sworn oath of police to serve the public at large confers on them an intrinsic legitimacy.

Two elements of the police mandate give power to this legitimacy. The first derives from the process by which officers are screened, trained, and then solemnly sworn to serve the public, which we have noted earlier.[51] The other, more significant, element derives from the fact that under the Constitution the police serve the state, the public at large, not specific individuals. A fundamental precept of this Adamsian government-of-laws-and-not-men notion is that it breeds impartiality.[52] Bayley and Shearing have noted that the great significance of public police in democratic nations is that they are "accountable to every citizen through the mechanisms of representative government" (1983, 596).

Private security personnel do not have such a broad and profound mandate. They have, however, been granted an *extrinsic* legitimacy by a clientele that has experienced limitations in the service of sworn police:

resource constraints for the provision of basic services, inability to provide various specialized services and products, and unreliable or otherwise insufficient responsiveness to particular needs. Privatization serves largely to complement public policing in the delivery of specialized services, but it has come to serve as a substitute as well, filling voids in basic service left by police departments that have been swamped by overwhelming demands and a variety of other sources of lapses in service delivery.

Ironically, the police have lost legitimacy the most in places where crime rates are highest and effective private alternatives are beyond affordability — the inner cities. Inner-city residents have experienced a multitude of lapses, originating in a lack of respect by the police and manifesting as the inconsistent application of force. Municipal police have too often acted far beyond the level appropriate to achieve compliance. Perhaps more often they have been completely unresponsive when some show or threat of force was needed. The community policing movement is showing signs of restoring some of this lost legitimacy to urban police departments (Skogan 1990; Kelling and Coles 1996).

❏ WHERE FROM HERE?

How can we use information about the evolution of modern policing and models for assessing policing services to design a system of policing for the twenty-first century? This will depend in part on what we think the future needs for those services will be. It will require also a detachment from preconceived notions that private alternatives are inherently superior to public, or vice versa. Both the public and private sectors have demonstrated more than ample capacities for ineffectiveness, waste, preferential treatment, and corruption.

Dubious Directions

Many of the contemporary prescriptions for improving public safety are clearly questionable. Cries for substantially more police are simultaneously among the most popular and most dubious of the recent solutions proposed for dealing with the problem of crime. Born largely of the widespread public misperception that crime rates are higher than ever before — an illusion that few politicians have either the courage or decency to dispel — these calls have led to such extraordinary measures as a $13 billion allocation of federal funds for police under the Crime Control Act of 1994. The funds have been tied in principle to the expansion of community policing activities, but the link is tenuous and difficult for the federal government to monitor and enforce. Complaints that the allocations of these funds are more closely related to political pork than to the expansion of specific community policing interventions have not been effectively refuted; much of the federal bounty goes to relatively well-financed, low-crime-rate areas. It is common practice for a police department to enlist a consultant from a nearby university or think tank to help fashion a proposal that suggests a substantive awareness of community policing and then to use the funds to finance whatever activity the police department actually cares to support. In flagrant cases the grant may not be renewed, but throughout the recent history of such federal largesse, U.S. Department of Justice attempts to recover the spent funds have been extremely rare.

A second dubious claim is based on skepticism of the market economy: that the profit motive of the private security industry is generally incompatible with the goals of policing — reduced crime and disorder, increased public safety.[53] What this argument lacks is a coherent justification, moral or otherwise, for the alleged incompatibility. How is it that the pursuit of satisfying the public's demand for security is more harmful when done for profit than when done through government? Can market imperfections in the delivery of such services — especially, inequitable distribution of police resources — be effectively dealt with? Do the social costs of those imperfections exceed the costs associated with inefficiencies that accompany monopoly in the governmental delivery of those services? Why is the activity of satisfying demands for security any less worthy of profit than that of, say, satisfying the demand for food, housing, clothing, or health care? Can the prospect of profit be viewed as benign compensation for the commitment of scarce capital resources and risk of financial loss and bankruptcy not faced by the public sector?

The Need for Public-Private Cooperation

There are, on the other hand, several promising avenues for improving policing generally and for responding to the demands raised by a burgeoning private security industry. One is in the area of coordination between public police and private security agents. At current rates of expansion in the respective sectors, one might expect some 800,000 sworn police officers and perhaps 2,500,000 contract guards and proprietary security forces by the year 2000. Given the vast coordination problems even among the 17,000 police departments in the United States, can we really expect personnel to learn to work effectively with one another across the ostensibly greater public-private divide?

The opportunities for mutual gains from improved coordination for both police and private security agencies are substantial, especially in the sharing of investigative expertise and intelligence information. Several promising developments suggest that an enlightened approach to cooperation between public and private police has already begun to take place in some quarters. In 1985 the New York Police Department formed a committee to look into the prospect of improved coordination with private security networks in the city. The result, the Area Police-Private Security Liaison Program, established a variety of working ties between the public and private domains (Voelker 1991):

1. The NYPD kept security directors informed about local crime trends and patterns, wanted persons, and lost/stolen property, information that was disseminated throughout the private security sector.
2. Private security directors, in turn, informed police about internal crimes, shared knowledge of plant and personnel protection, and advised the police of other pertinent on-site observations.
3. Police commanders and security directors met monthly, division managers met quarterly, and line police officers met informally at other times, often daily, with their private counterparts.
4. The NYPD routinely disseminated information about recent patterns of crime, along with sketches, photographs, and descriptions of active offenders.

These alliances appear to have improved working relations and mutual respect of the police and private security communities in New York. Several solved crimes have been attributed to these activities (Voelker 1991). Similar cooperative efforts have been reported in Dallas, Chicago, Tacoma, (Washington), and Montgomery County, Maryland (Williams 1991, 476).

Special problems of coordination present themselves in volatile circumstances in which the potential for large-scale disorder exists. Examples include security maintenance at the Olympic Games and dealing with the aftermath of police brutality, as in the case of the 1992 Los Angeles riots and the 1980 Miami riots (Skolnick and Fyfe 1993).

The handling of security at the 1996 Olympic Games in Atlanta was instructive. An estimated $227 million was allocated for a security force of some 30,000, comprised of 13,000 private guards, 8,500 military personnel, 4,800 state and local police officers, 2,500 federal agents, and 1,000 federal civilian employees.[54] The Atlanta Police Department's 1,500-person force, already saddled with the highest index crime rate among the nation's cities with populations over 100,000 and a scandal involving six officers convicted of taking bribes to protect drug dealers, was especially extended by the operation. When a 911 call warning of a bomb during the nighttime festivities at the densely populated Centennial Olympic Park area came to the police department at the end of the first week of the games, delays in getting the information to the various security agents responsible for clearing the area resulted in one death and over one hundred serious injuries. Within a few days FBI investigators singled out Richard Jewell, the security guard who had found the knapsack containing the bomb and had helped to clear out the area, as the prime suspect. After several months of intense scrutiny, Jewell was removed from suspicion as an official suspect. At the time of this writing, no other suspects have been arrested. There is surely room for disagreement over the conduct of this high-profile investigation. There appears to be little dispute, however, that improved coordination among the responsible agents could clearly have prevented such extensive human suffering and fear in the first place, as well as irresponsible leaks to the media that followed.[55]

Accreditation, Bonding, and Licensing

Many of the personnel working as private security agents and guards are inadequately screened, trained, and supervised to ensure effective police work. One solution to the need for improvements in the quality of both public and private policing services is to encourage accreditation in both domains. Precedents exist for both: the Commission on the Accreditation of Law Enforcement Agencies for police departments in the United States and the British Security Industry Association for the professionalization of the private security trade.

A related solution would be to require that private security firms carry general liability insurance, or that security personnel be bonded following a minimum level of training and certification, with the amount of training and size of bonding dependent on the degree of risk associated with the nature of the job.[56]

Others have suggested the prospect of licensing private security firms.[51] Most states currently license guard and patrol firms, and about half require the registration of guards.[58] James Jacobs has observed that existing licensing institutions are under-resourced and ineffective; license revocations are extremely rare. He warns that more restrictive licensing provisions would impose costs that would be passed on to the consumer, making private security services even less accessible to poor citizens than they already are (1983, 1141). Economists have long noted that licensing arrangements juried by prevailing experts in the field in the name of protecting consumers typically do more to serve producers by restricting market entry. The licensing solution thus presents a time-worn conundrum that transcends policing: Can licensing arrangements be devised that improve the quality of private services without making them less affordable?

Dealing with Moonlighters

Many sworn police officers work part-time in security positions. Though many departments prohibit such arrangements,[60] some 150,000 police officers moonlight as private security agents.[61] These officers are better trained than most of the alternatively hired guards, but special problems do arise when the establishments where these officers work part-time are in the officer's full-time police jurisdiction: risk of corruption, questions of liability (especially coverage for injury and sick leave), conflict of interests and favoritism, problems of reduced effectiveness on official duty as a result of energy consumed by private workloads, and questions about whether uniforms, publicly issued resources, and publicly financed training should be used for the benefit of private interests. (Senna and Siegel 1993; Stewart 1985)

What distinguishes police from the members of every other public institution is that we give them the unique power to use coercive force in situations in which, according to Egon Bittner, "Something-ought-not-to-be-happening-about-which-something-ought-to-be-done-NOW!" (1974, 30).[62] Moonlighting may compound the already fragile ability of police to use this power wisely by serving to deter sworn officers from curbing the excesses of private police. Those who lack resources to buy their own private police may lose all faith in sworn officers who cannot respond to the complaint, "You're the police. Why aren't you protecting me from this rent-a-cop?"[63]

Inner-City Redevelopment and Public Safety

The wholesale flight of businesses from inner cities that accelerated in the late 1960s and early 1970s was due primarily to the fears, risks, and extraordinary costs associated with the explosion of crime during that period. The prospect of a return of commerce to those areas depends no less on increased levels of protection, public and private. One would expect two developments to be critical for such protection: (1) that municipal police departments decentralize their operations so that sworn officers have the autonomy to identify the specific needs of each area for which they are responsible, and (2) that some substantial portion of the business development created, perhaps under some sort of enterprise-zone arrangement,[64] would consist of private security institutions — for-profit, nonprofit, and volunteer — to preserve and protect the return of wholesome living conditions in our urban centers. Such developments could be essential for the redevelopment of our inner cities, regardless of how the redevelopment is facilitated.

The Emergence of Communitarian Alternatives

One development that may bode well not only for policing but for meeting many contemporary challenges is the recent growth of communitarian alternatives to social problems. Spawned by the writings of Amitai Etzioni (1988, 1993), Mary Ann Glendon (1991), Jane Mansbridge (1990), and others, the communitarian movement emphasizes limitations in both governmental and market solutions to many vexing issues of public policy; it explores solutions that blend the strengths of each major sector, including the building of partnerships between public and private groups and experimentation with the creative use of various forms of cooperation (Etzioni et al. 1991). While many have bemoaned the apparent decline of civic engagement (Putnam 1991), others have noted that declines in certain areas (participation in bowling leagues, Little League baseball, League of Women Voters, garden clubs) have been offset by gains in others (participation in adult baseball and children's soccer leagues, neighborhood blockwatch programs) (Stengel 1996).

Centerpieces of the communitarian agenda include inducements to volunteer work, the emphasis on a sense of responsibility and deemphasis on a sense of rights, and wider use of informal social sanctions to induce ethical behavior: shame as a stick and positive reinforcements as carrots to encourage community-minded behavior. The communitarian manifesto holds that "our first and foremost purpose is to *affirm the moral commitments of parents, young persons, neighbors, and citizens* . . . If communities are to function well, most members most of the time must discharge their responsibilities because they committed to do so, not because they fear lawsuits, penalties or jails."[65]

Though these notions do not resolve questions about the optimal mix of public and private solutions to problems of crime and community order, they do suggest a commonsense framework for addressing such matters. Public and private solutions to specific crime problems may occasionally ignore larger community interests, but if they are not complemented by systematic and purposeful activities that build community participation, they will do little to achieve larger crime prevention and order maintenance goals. The police will be more effective when they have succeeded in building positive ties to the community, including private security agents working for individuals and institutions within the community. They can work to encourage citizens to protect themselves in crime prevention and to provide information to the police to facilitate the solving of crimes. Private security agents are responsible primarily to those who pay for their services. One cannot expect those agents to take the lead in community building. It is not unreasonable, however, to ask their patrons to be mindful of the external benefits and costs of the behaviors of these security agents; if they are not, court litigation may fill the void.

Conclusion

Is privatization good or bad? Do we need more privatization of policing or less? If we have learned anything, it is that such questions are too simplistic to warrant serious answers.

This much is clear: The notion that either our corps of sworn police officers or the expanding array of private security agents alone is uniquely equipped to protect society and maintain order without the other is an idea without credible support. Neither the public nor the private sector is endowed with attributes that ensure that policing in either domain will be automatically superior to the alternative in every respect. Neither has revealed the capacity to respond effectively to the variety of social trends that characterize our contemporary landscape, trends that suggest the inevitability of more crime and disorder in many segments of society — demographics, increased use of guns by adolescents, the decline of family, expanded exposure of youth to violence, and vast disparities in education and wealth.

It is nonetheless likely that recent trends in policing will continue for some time to come, in spite of questions about their appropriateness to emerging social problems. As we enter the twenty first century, with substantial increases in store in both the absolute and relative size of the population in the crime-prone ages of fifteen to twenty-four, it is doubtful that each major segment of our society can be adequately served by current methods of policing, public and private. As society changes, so must policing.

Acceptable solutions to satisfying the public's needs for security are bound to consist of a widely varied mix of public and private alternatives: sworn officers, civilians working in police departments, private firms hired under contract by police departments and municipal governments to serve well-defined security and support needs, subsidies for poor people to have access to resources that make their environments safer, security guards and specialists hired to protect commercial interests, citizens serving voluntarily to protect their communities, typically in coordination with the police, and citizens augmenting and substituting public protection with a broad range of goods and services to protect private property and provide personal protection. Such a panoply of options working simultaneously are virtually certain to fill gaps in service that more limited alternatives cannot accomplish.

Debate over the appropriate mix of options, a mix that adequately satisfies the extraordinary variety of the public's security needs, has been too often contaminated by deep faith in either governmental or market solutions, combined with equally deep suspicion of the other sector.[66] A more coherent and effective resolution is likely to result from thoughtful consideration of the extent to which each option contributes to each aspect of our need for security — in terms of how effective, how equitable, and how economical, it is and the extent to which it permits freedom of choice.

The great contemporary challenge confronting public safety in the United States is not primarily to decide whether privatization is a good thing. It is to find a way to shape and coordinate our resources and energies to secure the safety of those quarters of society that are least able to afford effective security, public or private. Wealthy communities can afford to take care of themselves both publicly and privately, and they do so. Poor people, especially minorities living in areas with the highest concentrations of crime, cannot. Sworn police officers must be made available in sufficient numbers and with effective systems of accountability to ensure that those areas are adequately served and protected.

The 1980s were marked by intense suspicion of the ability of governments to adequately respond to public needs and by often-blind faith in market solutions. The 1990s have witnessed a search for more eclectic solutions to matters of public and private policy, approaches that emphasize voluntarism and greater cooperation among institutions in the public and private sectors. The popularity of the community policing strategies in municipal police departments in cities throughout the democratic world is a hopeful manifestation of this enlightened spirit of partnership. Such approaches to maintaining domestic peace and order appear to be more open to diverse and flexible responses to problems of public policy and to a style of policing that may be both more humane and more effective. This trend is likely, in any case, to induce a healthier debate and in turn produce superior solutions for the coming millenium.

NOTES

1. This is a shortened version of the actual joke. The full version includes a respondent from a fourth country often lampooned for the rudeness of some of its citizens and the question, "Excuse me, what is your opinion of the beef shortage?" The fourth respondent asks, "What is 'excuse me'?"

2. Egon Bittner (1970): Bittner's distinction follows Max Weber's (1954) characterization of the state as the institution that holds a monopoly of legitimate use of violence in the area under its control.

3. Trivia: "Pinkerton's agents" is the answer to Paul Newman's question "Who are those guys?" — asked as his character, Butch Cassidy, was fleeing from an especially persistent band of pursuers in the movie *Butch Cassidy and the Sundance Kid*.

4. P.K. Manning (1995) describes the continuing use of effectiveness measures as a triumph of rhetoric over substance and, more fundamentally, a triumph of managerial economics over public administration: "These changes in policing, especially the metaphoric tendency whereby policing is conceived as an economic institution, are part of the overall movement toward privatization of control, reduction of government supervision in favor of the market and private governments, and the use of the media and the market to substitute symbolic imagery for direct forceful authority. The present appeal to market forces for reform, analogous to deregulation, is a retrograde step with regard to civic control over police command and police accountability" (p. 382).

5. Patrick V. Murphy, New York City Police Commissioner in the early 1970s, referred to this distance as "stranger policing . . . the occupation of conquered territory by an alien army." Murphy elaborated that under stranger policing, "it is permissible for officers to hide in their radio cars with windows rolled up, communicating not with the community but only with each other, the dispatchers at headquarters, and their own private thoughts" (Deakin 1988, p.231).

6. Much of this was a product of increased administrative demands and more time in court. Savas (1982) observes, however, that much was due to effective union pressure; while the New York Police Department grew from 16,000 to 24,000 officers over a recent twenty-five-year period, the total hours worked actually declined, largely because of increases in leave and vacation time (p. 24).

7. Akerlof and Yellin (1994) have noted that the police have mostly alienated inner-city residents, that gangs have been more successful than the police in winning over the hearts and minds of many urban minority communities. Akerlof and Yellin's work is significant for providing a coherent theoretical framework for community policing.

8. Judith Martin's (1996) observation is instructive:

> Between them, etiquette and law divide the task of regulating social conduct in the interest of community harmony, with the law addressing grave conflicts, such as those threatening life or property, and administering serious punishments, while etiquette seeks to forestall such conflicts, relying on voluntary compliance with its restraints . . . The danger of attempting to expand the dominion of the law to take over the function of etiquette — to deal with such violations as students calling one another nasty names, or protesters doing provocative things with flags — is that it may compromise our constitutional rights. For all its strictness, a generally understood community standard of etiquette is more flexible than the law and, because it depends on voluntary compliance, less threatening . . . That we cannot live peacefully in communities without etiquette, using only the law to prevent or resolve conflicts in everyday life, has become increasingly obvious to the public. (P. 55–56)

9. See Elliott (1991, 62). Cunningham, et al. (1990) found that specific policing tasks were performed more efficiently by less costly private security agents: guarding public buildings, enforcing parking regulations, and maintaining court security. Similarly, Benson (1998) reports substantial improvements in the recovery of bad checks when the Kentwood (Michigan) Police Department contracted out the investigation of bad checks to private agents.

10. Colby (1995, 121–22) has reported that municipalities in Los Angeles County and Cook County (Chicago) have also contracted with their respective county sheriff's departments for policing services at lower costs.

11. Senna and Siegel (1993) report such results for Reminderille, Ohio (p. 234); Elliott (1991) reports similar results for Oro Valley, Arizona, and Kalamazoo, Michigan (p. 62). Walsh and Donovan (1989) report increased levels of safety, reduced levels of fear, and improved quality of life with private security services over public police services for Starrett City, a residential community of forty six high-rise buildings in Brooklyn, New York (p. 187). "Substantial savings" were reported in *Urban Innovation Abroad* (1980) following the contracting of police services in some thirty villages and townships in Switzerland. Hilke's 1992 survey of over one hundred studies of privatization generally found cost reductions in the 20 percent to 50 percent range.

12. Mangan and Shanahan estimate about 2,000,000 members of private security organizations in 1990; the Bureau of Justice Statistics estimates some 650,000 police officers for the same year (*Sourcebook of Criminal Justice Statistics* 1991) By the mid-1990s, Sears employed 6,000 security guards (Office of International Criminal Justice 1995), more than the Los Angeles Police Department had sworn officers. Laband and Sophocleus (1992) estimate total private-sector spending on protection against crime at $300 billion annually, about three times the amount spent on the entire public criminal justice system.

Nalla and Newman (1991) have noted that comparisons of private and public personnel are flawed by definitional questions: Which categories of private security personnel should be included? Which categories of police personnel? Sworn officers only? They argue that including state and federal tax collectors and regulators in the public police numbers produces less divergent assessments.

13. See McDonald (1992, 378). As with the publicization of policing, prisoners were held in private facilities in England and elsewhere in Europe until the nineteenth century (p. 379).

14. The latter variable is important for limiting spuriousness in the findings for the other variables: laws restricting patronage, unionization, public spending, and so on. Lopez de Silanes, Shleifer, and Vishny (1985) find that the effect of the last variable is fairly small: an additional 10 percent of voters for the Republican gubernatorial candidate is associated with a 1.1 percent increase in the probability that a public service will be contracted out. Changes in the other variables analyzed tended to reveal substantially larger effects on privatization.

15. Examples include a faction of Oakland's Black Panthers that sought to provide armed private security services to the community in the late 1960s, and men loyal to Louis Farrakhan in Washington, D.C., in the mid-1990s. See Akerlof and Yellin (1994) for a discussion of the issues associated with the competition between police departments and gangs for control of inner-city communities.

16. The law in most states stipulates that private persons are authorized to make arrests only in the case of felonies that occur in their presence (Jacobs 1983, 1140). More generally, the Supreme Court has not acted to constrain state and local governments from delegating powers to private agents since 1920 (McDonald 1992, 406); it allowed the federal government to delegate broad powers to private actors in its decision in *Carter v. Carter Coal Company*, 298 U.S. 238 (1936).

17. Vice President Gore's sentiments are not unprecedented. The 1955 Office of Management and Budget Circular A-76 states that "it has been and continues to be the general policy of the government to rely on competitive private enterprise to supply products and services it needs."

18. The Congressional Budget Office has estimated that $1 billion could be saved over a five-year period by replacing the construction of new public housing with a system of vouchers; a HUD official estimates that the vouchers would also expand by some 300,000 units the stock of housing options available to current public housing tenants (Hage et al. 1995, 44).

19. Privatization has been stimulated by government withdrawals from, or breakdowns in, other sectors as well. Education is a conspicuous example.

20. Johnston (1992, 55) observes that many public police agencies protect not only ineffective sworn officers but large, often inefficient civilian staffs as well.

21. Because governmental accounting convention treats the full cost of a capital outlay as an expenditure in the year incurred rather than as an investment whose cost is spread over the life of the asset, the public sector tends to underinvest in capital resources. Public resources are inefficiently allocated also in year-end use-it-or-lose-it spending binges of authorized government budgets.

22. Although systematic evidence of actual successes has not yet been well documented, community policing aims specifically to overcome this problem in large municipal police departments. A prominent example of a specific, well-defined goal of private security is that of corporate loss prevention. A company's director of security or loss prevention is typically held accountable to a straightforward bottom-line criterion: the reduction in theft and safety losses to the company should exceed the marginal costs associated with those reductions to an extent that exceeds the company's standard rate of return on investments (Becker 1995, 655–56).

23. Sherman (1995, 339) notes that public police once exercised trespass powers illegally, especially in small communities where offenders could be run out of town; they rarely do so today.

24. Many police departments exploit such economies by contracting out specific services, often to multiple private contractors.

25. McCrie (1988, 32) notes that while individual police departments tend to monopolize local law enforcement markets, among some 13,500 private security firms in the United States, no single firm controls as much as 10 percent of the market.

26. 367 U.S. 643 (1961).

27. However, the reverse may hold when the services of private agents are contracted by public authorities. Under *West v. Atkins,* 487 U.S. 42, 55 (1988), private parties may become state actors when their activities violating constitutional rights are authorized, encouraged, or approved by the government. Moreover, public servants receive certain constitutional immunities against civil suits not generally available to private agents (Rosenbloom 1998, 6–7). Rosenbloom argues that such asymmetry may have a chilling effect on the willingness of private agents to act on behalf of the state (pp. 14–15).

28. Manning (1995a) summarizes these considerations in identifying one of the postulates of the police culture as follows: "The legal system is untrustworthy; policemen make the best decisions about guilt or innocence" (p. 102).

29. Nozick (1974, 12) has observed that the "morally objectionable" transactions that give rise to overly aggressively private protection providers may thus induce a return to the state's monopoly control over protection.

30. See Williams (1991, 475). The same problem has been known in the hiring of public officers as well, as in the case of the notorious hiring binge of the District of Columbia's Metropolitan Police Department in 1989–90.

31. Private security agencies have two strong incentives *not* to arm their employees: heightened liability risks and higher insurance premiums when their guards are armed. One of the largest private security firms, Guardsmark, estimated that just 3 percent of its uniformed personnel were armed in 1985 (Cunningham and Taylor 1985a, 20).

32. Kakalik and Wildhorn (1977) found that most of the security guards they sampled were unaware that their arrest powers were no greater than those of an ordinary citizen. Most had received less than two days of training prior to taking responsibility in their assigned positions.

33. Skolnick and Fyfe (1993) make the point effectively:

Cops are not supposed to be security guards on the public payroll who, like bouncers in a rough-and-tumble bar, are on hand to mete out punishment as they see fit. Rather, in a free society, especially in the United States, where police derive their authority from law and take an oath to support the Constitution, they are obliged to acknowledge the law's moral force and to be constrained by it. Any sensible and reflective police officer will understand that when a cop reaches above the law to use more force or coercion than is necessary to subdue a suspect, he or she undermines the very source of police authority. (P.xvi)

34. This is not to suggest that private security agents have generally lower levels of commitment to service. Many bank guards, Brinks and Wells Fargo drivers, and other private security agents have given their lives in the service of protecting others.

35. Equally regrettably, it may contribute to posturing and feigning of virtuous intent as a cover for less noble purposes. Frequent revelations of corrupt behaviors of people sworn to public service generally and to protecting the public in particular have bred a widespread cynicism that has done vast harm to the image of public servants and public service institutions.

36. The author, Howard Shook, is former president of the International Association of Chiefs of Police.

37. In a similar vein, P. K. Manning (1995b) dismisses economic constructs as symbolic, devoid of substance; the "economic metaphor" is little more than a construct of 1980s Republicanism:

The economic metaphor for policing and police reform has emerged in the last ten years and is consistent with the economic philosophy of the Reagan-Bush administrations. It urges one to think of policing in terms of supply and demand, and in market-competitive terms. From this perspective policing is viewed as a "service," a distributional activity that serves to reallocate collective goods. (P. 388)

38. See, for example, Stewart (1985, 762); Sparrow et al. (1990, 49).

39. Gross domestic product in the United States was $6.74 trillion in 1994, 67.3 percent of which consisted of private consumption expenditures; $1.18 trillion (17.4 percent was consumed by the government sector and $1.03 trillion (15.3 percent) consisted of gross domestic investment. *Encyclopedia Britannica: 1996 Book of the Year;* S.V.

40. Demsetz (1970) argues that indivisibility of benefits need not impede the private production and delivery of public goods, leaving nonexcludability as the sole distinguishing characteristic of public goods.

41. Arthur Kellerman et al. (1993) have found that these costs may substantially outweigh the security benefits of gun ownership. They report that the likelihood of death due to either homicide, accidental or otherwise, or suicide is on the order of four times higher in homes with guns than in homes without guns, other factors held constant.

42. The police impose external diseconomies as well — for example, in injuring innocent people in car chases. Moreover, external diseconomies imposed by both types of police are partly offset by external economies. I may feel safer either when my neighborhood is known to have protected itself or when a police precinct is just around the corner.

43. Privatization that grants exclusive rights to a particular security agent is less likely to yield gains in efficiency than other types of privatization, since a primary purpose of privatization is to derive the benefits of competition. Replacing government monopoly with private monopoly fails by this fundamental standard.

44. I am grateful to James Lynch for pointing out the importance of geography in the segmentation of public and private policing.

45. Landes and Posner (1975), focusing on efficiency rather than equity and choice, have argued that society tends to rely on public enforcement more in cases where the cost of enforcing an individual claim is high relative to the value of the claim, and that, in general, these matters tend to sort themselves out automatically: "Society has left enforcement to the private sector in areas where private enforcement is clearly optimal" (p. 32).

46. Miethe (1991) reports finding that homes are unaffected one way or the other by the existence of an immediate neighbor's alarm system.

47. Hakim and Buck (1991) have estimated that about 95 percent of all alarm activations are false. False alarms accounted for some 15 percent of all dispatches of squad cars in New York City in 1981; 98 percent of those calls were false (Cunningham et al. 1990).

48. See Hakim et al. (1996). Flusty (1994), focusing on declining aesthetics in Los Angeles, puts it more dramatically:

> Expanding private encroachment into the public realm is catering to, and exacerbating, paranoid demands by gradually decomposing communities into fortified agglomerations of proprietary spaces. In the process, sections of the city have become a patchwork of contiguous interdictory spaces, subjecting citizens' mobility and permissible range of behavior to ever more restrictive oversight and control. The cumulative spatial and aesthetic effects of paranoid privatization are already being manifested across broad landscapes, turning the streets into prickly space hemmed in by crusty and slippery edges . . . . In short, Los Angeles is undergoing the invention and installation, component by component, of physical infrastructure engendering electronically linked islands of privilege embedded in a police state matrix. (Pp. 34, 36)

49. Hakim et al. (1996, pp. 164–65) report that the benefits to a small township in 1990 exceeded the costs by a "conservative estimate" of over $200 per installed home security system.

50. Hakim et al. (1996, p. 159) estimate the average 1996 cost of each false alarm in Tredyffrin Township, in southeastern Pennsylvania, at about $70.

51. The sacred vow of service is akin to that taken by medieval knights to the empires they served. See Wambaugh's *Blue Knights* for further parallels. One significant difference is that knights' vows were sworn primarily to their kings rather than to the empire.

52. The notion did not originate with John Adams. The following is from Aristotle (1943): "A social instinct is implanted in all men by nature, and yet he who first founded the state was the greatest of benefactors. For man, when perfected, is the best of animals, but, when separated from law and justice, he is the worst of all" 1948, (p. 55). Note also that the word "police" is rooted in Greek governance; it relates today to the enforcement of laws established through a democratic *political* process.

53. See, for example, Shearing and Stenning (1981). Shearing (1992) adds to these notions the specter of "giant corporations . . . sites of governance" operating in global markets that "challeng[e] the boundaries of states and the very notion of the state as a basis for political organization" (p. 425). In a similar vein, Flusty (1994) asserts, "As with most private enterprises, supranational corporations (SNCs) are autocratic organizations accountable to profitability and, at most, to select shareholders" (p. 38).

A related claim is that society would be better off if police resources were shifted from the prevention and control of street crime to that of white-collar crime. Though such claims are often supported by utilitarian arguments that the costs of white-collar crime are much greater than those associated with street crime, they appear to be born not so much of utilitarian concerns as of an egalitarian concern that it is fundamentally unjust for public resources to target street offenders while crimes committed by the more affluent are largely ignored. Posner (1972 376–79) observes that fewer of these crimes would go unpunished if government restrictions against private enforcement were relaxed

54. Data from the Atlanta Committee for the Olympic Games, reported by Boeck and Lynn (1996).

55. This was but one serious problem facing the Atlanta Police Department. Another was the department's focus on the Olympic sites, which took officers off the streets — contributing to colossal traffic jams that made athletes, journalists, and spectators late to competitions. The problem was exacerbated by the department's allowing vendors to clog sidewalks, forcing pedestrians onto the streets for passage (Heath 1996).

56. Cunningham and Taylor (1985a) note that several states already require that security firms carry general liability insurance or bonding insurance.

57. See, for example, Stewart (1985, 764).

58. Bureau of Justice Statistics (1988, 66).

59. Adam Smith ([1776] 1937) observed over two hundred years ago: "People of the same trade seldom meet together, even for merriment and diversion, but the conversation ends in a conspiracy against the public, or in some contrivance to raise prices" (P. 128).

60. Reiss (1988, p. 80) estimates that some 20 percent of all police departments prohibit moonlighting.

61. Reiss (1988, p. 9). Cory (1979, 40) also reports results of a 1975 study of Cleveland: between 20 and 35 percent of the local police officers were found to work second jobs in private security.

62. See also Klockars, (1985, 16).

63. I thank Jim Lynch for this point.

64. The enterprise-zone concept is a proposal for improving the quality of life in our inner cities. Popularized by former Congressman Jack Kemp in 1980, the basic idea is to use the market economy to restore vibrancy to areas that once thrived commercially and culturally, through two primary vehicles: tax credits to facilitate capital investments and the elimination of regulations that needlessly restrict commerce in poor areas. The concept has been supported by both ends of the political spectrum, from former President Ronald Reagan to Harlem Democrat Charles Rangel. Its success depends, perhaps more than anything else, on stable social organization (Sviridoff 1994).

65. Etzioni et al. (1991, 11) (emphasis in the original). Etzioni views deontology — importance of duty — as the essential philosophical foundation of communitarianism (1988, 12).

66. Drucker (1995) observes that the amount or size of government is not the central issue:

> We need *effective government* . . . For this, however, we need something we do not have: a theory of what government can do. No major political thinker — at least not since Machiavelli, almost 500 years ago — has addressed this question. All political theory, from Locke on through *The Federalist Papers* and down to the articles published by today's liberals and conservatives, deals with the process of government: with constitutions, with power and its limitations, with methods and organizations. None deals with the substance. None asks what the proper functions of government might be and could be. None asks what results government should be held accountable for. (P. 61)

PART TWO

Peter K. Manning
A Dramaturgical Perspective

❏ AN OVERVIEW OF POLICING

This part of the book adumbrates the relationships between private and public policing, with a contemporaneous focus: what are the consequences, anticipated and known, of the "privatization of police functions"? To discuss this, it is necessary to address the nature of policing in general, the dialectic between public and private forms of policing, and the current ideological climate. My argument in brief is that policing is fundamentally rooted in coercion and violence and is ill suited to reform based on modern managerial economics — in part because of the historical practices that sustain policing as an occupation and its divisions — and that questions of efficiency, effectiveness, distribution of services, and even the quality and quantity of service cannot be easily shaped by economic rhetoric and managerial practice. Furthermore, the fundamentally sacred nature of policing, its connection to social order and social solidarity, means that it is primordial, a fundamental building block of the state's power and legitimacy, and resistant to reform and to reorganization. To address the police with questions of modern institutional economics is to speak to an early-nineteenth-century institution with twenty-first-century language. In short, the police remain primitive, archaic, collective, and even sacred because they represent the core of inarticulated desires, order, and power; they must be controlled and controlling.

A pervasive crisis, manifesting itself in policing generally, suggests that policing, both public and private, be reexamined, and that cross-organizational generalizations be sought. Certainly, private security should be scrutinized to the same extent that researchers have examined public policing beginning in the sixties. There are two sides to my discussion here: a *primary theme*, the impact of "privatization" on public police, and a *secondary theme,* changes within private policing as a result of the changing mandate of public police and perhaps of policing in general.

Part 2 will not provide a brief history of forms of policing (see Radzinowicz 1948–1966, Johnston 1992) or develop a full framework for the analysis of police work (see P.K. Manning 1997).[1] My aim is more modest. To address the questions presented by policing in the twenty-first century, especially how it is to respond to modern market forces, we must examine privatization, definitions, and functions of policing; the crisis emerging in both public and private policing; and the prospects for policing in the twenty-first century. We will also address some dilemmas and contradictions associated with these issues.

Privatization

One of the most misleading assumptions in the study of policing is the notion that policing denotes public policing, and that privatization proceeds from the ostensible monopoly of the public police. To label these changes "privatization" suggests a one-way process by which public police, having controlled all policing functions, are now delegating, mandating, or giving them up to other agencies. This incorrectly implies that the public police have existed as something of a legitimate monopoly, that this monopoly is now attenuating, and that functions are being sloughed off exclusively in one direction. In simple terms, the idea of privatization sees influence as unidirectional. Market forces, whether seen as good or evil, serve to commodify security, and this affects both a broadening of private security and public agencies. Both are responsible for the collective good in practice. Both public and private police are subject to market pressures and changing.

Logically, privatization assumes income generation or redistribution once money has been deemed public. As Forst points out in Part 1, the idea can refer to a variety of mechanisms for distributing public spending or production or revenue raising, and can be evaluated by a number of standards, largely economic, such as the impact of these mechanisms on choice, quality and quantity of services, or equity in distribution. The terms of reference initially are economic, although the process raises questions that are studied by researchers in public administration, political science, economics, anthropology, and sociology. The rhetoric of economics, and perhaps law and economics, now dominates public policy debate in this country (Moore 1995).

Exploring privatization of policing, as with all complex questions, requires delimitation and definition, but the questions remain rooted in the context of justice in the broadest sense because in a democracy issues regarding freedom of choice, quality of services, and distribution have become defined as utilitarian. These are central questions because the police not only represent justice and the state but are also engaged in ordering and governance that shape the distribution of symbolic goods, life opportunities, and well-being. Further, they dispense coercion and are at the heart of the legitimacy of the state. Their responsibilities include maintaining the governmentally defined status quo. Many questions asked in the privatization debate are pragmatic or arise from economics — questions of utility, efficiency, responsibility, skills, and training — rather than dealing with the nature of risks to the collective good or the means by which it is best sustained.[2] Questions of comparative efficiency, effectiveness, and value-added functions, or even the gross costs of policing functions, cannot be addressed because data are unavailable. Even the always negotiated and symbolic bottom line, — profit versus loss — is difficult to apply to functions that aim to prevent and manage rather than to punish or sanction. Symbolic matters such as good name, credibility, and integrity are essential to policing, but they are subtle notions. What is the value to a corporation of a prevented assault or hostage situation, a foiled kidnapping of an executive who need not be ransomed by a company, secrets retained and not stolen by competitors, or losses due to dissatisfaction and low turnover among employees? For these reasons, very little empirical data are available for systematic comparative analysis of private security, and analogous gaps exist in the evaluation of policing generally.

How shall the public best be policed? To whom are police accountable and for what? The task of our dialogue is not to predict the future of policing, but rather to identify the limits and dilemmas of the process of change and privatization.

To address the impact of changes in policing, both public and private, one must consider research and definitions. As the following chapters show, the definitional problem remains unresolved.

Focus: Dialectic

I want to consider policing as a form of social control that expands and contracts and includes two types, private policing and public policing.

Private Policing

Private policing until recently has not been receptive to systematic social research.[3] Much of what has been done concerns general policy issues.[4] Published materials are pragmatic, utilitarian, ahistorical, atheoretical, and anti-intellectual. Much of what passes for research consists of slick and successful case studies, although the *Security Journal* and the American Association of Industrial Security (ASIS) encourage careful empirical studies by economists, criminologists, practitioners, and students of business administration. There are sound reasons for this, as much as one might wish it otherwise.

Private policing is protected by law and tradition from many of the constraints that vex public police (e.g., procedural limits on searches, surveillance, and access to private places). It guards information on its profits and costs carefully, is inclined to self-promotion and marketing, and borrows prestige and legitimacy by hiring retired CIA, FBI, Secret Service, and state police officers. Many ex-police hold executive positions in private security firms after retirement (Johnston 1992, 108). Imagery and corporate concern for profits limit information sharing and publication of bad news. Definitions of profit and loss are controlled by management, and data on the costs of corporate functions outside security divisions are unavailable to them. For example, estimates of the number of employees in the security "industry" (since it does not produce a product it is not really an industry) disagreement exists about classification of "security" and methods of sampling those so employed. Cunningham and Taylor (1985) question the sampling methods used by the Census Bureau to report estimates of the private security labor force. M. Nalla and G. Newman (1993, 44), using Shearing and Stenning's (1983) and the *Hallcrest* (Cunningham and Taylor 1985) estimates, show that private security employees exceed public police (with federal agencies omitted); this trend has continued since 1975, when it was estimated last that public employees exceeded private, that both show a steady increase, and that the current ratio slightly favors private security. As Forst notes in Part 1, debate continues about the expenditure on private security by individuals and corporations, the number of firms in the field, and the future. Unfortunately, some of these ambiguities remain in the public side as well.

Public Policing

Public policing in America is decentralized, uncoupled from central authority, and locally funded. It is estimated that some 15,1118 departments exist. The distribution by size shows a mode of small departments with an average size of 30 serving a population of around 15,000 people. On the other hand, 20 percent of serving officers are in the twenty-five largest departments — those with more than 3,800 officers (Bayley 1992a, 516). The 15,118 number includes 11,989 local forces, 3,080 county sheriffs, and 49 state police forces (Bayley 1992a, 512). Justice system costs in 1985 probably exceeded 50 billion dollars (Cunningham and Taylor 1985), may be five or six times that now, and are highlighted by the 12-billion dollar "war on drugs" and the 1994 Safe Streets and Omnibus crime bill, which is expected to pour more than 8.8 billion dollars (over several years) into criminal justice. This includes a program to add 100,000 officers administered through the COPS (Community Oriented Police Services) office.

The figures and costs are always at least partially notional because policing is loosely tied to direct market forces. Policing budgets are affected by crime and the economy, and the emergence of new forms of crime — computer crime, violations of trust using information networks, industrial espionage, terrorism, and drug-related crimes — has added to crime-control costs. Policing costs are expanded by demands for new information technologies, networking, and even basic computer hardware (terminals, printers, mainframe access, or local servers) as well as yearly updates in software (Reaves 1996; Reaves and Smith 1996). Other evidence suggests cost reductions could be realized by attrition through retirement, which could affect 20 percent of law enforcement in the next ten years, when combined with hiring younger officers and civilians (Bayley 1994, 90).

To evaluate the costs of policing, policing must be defined. Bear in mind that this is a discussion not just of *public* policing, but of *policing*. Joining the debate over the privatization of policing does not require a defense of one system or the other but concerns functions and emphases that cross apparent boundaries.

Definitions

Police, a word of Greek origin that refers in general to modes of internally regulating, governing, and administering civic life, connotes politics, the distribution of power and authority (Stead 1977, 1). It is an elusive term, and as Cain (1979) first pointed out, no systematic definition is adopted by researchers. The *Encyclopedia of Police Science* (Bailey 1995) contains no definition of the term (see, however, Bayley 1985, ch. 1). Policing is a controversial topic, whether one refers to public policing, which emerged in 1829–55 in Anglo-American democracies (Silver 1967), to variations in policing (state, county, federal agencies), to forms of private policing (Shearing 1992), or to self-help (Black 1983, 1984). Policing, on the one hand, is associated with notions like peace (Shearing 1992), peace of mind and peacekeeping, security, order and ordering (Shearing, Stenning 1983; Reiner 1992), and even medieval notions such as honor, chivalry, and duty (Bittner 1970; P.K. Manning 1997). On the other hand, policing is associated with violence, disorder, crime, and deviance. It produces fear, dread, and death.

The most common textbook approach to defining policing is to circumvent the issue by presenting an acontextual list of police functions (LaFave, 1967). Although Bittner's definition is sometimes offered in texts, it is presented almost in passing, without reference to its elegant, radical phenomenological, nonlegalistic, and situational imagery. Flaws in the definition considered below are rarely addressed. Bittner (1970, 39) defines police as "a mechanism for the distribution of situationally justified force in society." The police are required to stand ready to respond to all sorts of human problems when it is imagined that the application of force may be necessary at some point (44). Bittner adds, "The role of the police is best understood as a mechanism for the distribution of non-negotiably coercive force employed in accordance with the dictates of an intuitive grasp of situational exigencies" (46). The elements of this definition, its situational aspects, its focus on violence, its emphasis on an "intuitive grasp," and the absence of an explicit a priori legal dimension, convey penetrating insights.

The police are dangerous, a threat on the one hand to citizens and on the other to the state apparatus because they possess the license to use fatal force. In a modern welfare state this violence potential means that the state can and will act toward itself (in the form of the citizens who constitute it) in a violent and punitive fashion. Violence contains the seeds of its own unraveling. Police accountability remains ambiguous at law and by tradition.

Policing cannot be defined totally by its potential legitimate use of force, since it shares that with many organizations and an armed citizenry in the United States. Conversely, many of its functions are inspectorial, also shared with many other agencies, and linked to governance in general. Thus, policing must be defined necessarily by the legitimate use of force, but this in itself is not an adequate definition (Reiss, 1992a).

Although violence and its application are fundamental to police work, they are not definitive or exclusively the domain of policing. Police neither hold a monopoly on violence nor are the only organizations that enforce laws with that option in hand. While police work is potentially violent, in a democracy police are judged by the absence, not the presence, of violence. Policing must also display and realize the appearance of justice. Justice should be seen to be done. Mass societies require mass dramas, spectacles at the extreme, because so much experience is mediated experience, cast in the language of tension, conflict, and drama, and includes scenes we have never experienced directly. The police, public and private, are engaged in dramas which they direct, stage, perform in, and realize but cannot fully anticipate or alter. Policing functions are carried out by many agencies, public and private, but named police organizations are constrained by their mandate, imagery, and role in the division of labor.

Though the police are required to apply violence, they must do this within the constraints of a democratic polity and must be seen to be acting justly. "Being seen" means being vulnerable to being featured on television worldwide almost with minutes of an event. Policing, whatever else it might be, is dramatic; it is marked and stands out from everyday life.

The role of the police, as seen in Bittner's definition, focused on the situational application of force, is embedded in patterns or variations in social organization, socialization, and policing tradition. For most scholars, documenting and measuring aspects of the workings of police organizations, and describing their authority, dramatic potential, and realization, suffice. We return to this issue in the next section.

"Policing" is an important term in discourse and in everyday life because it has two faces: it shows order and peace and disorder and fear. This powerful two-sidedness entails the activities of individuals serving interests of both self and family as well as formally organized forms of control that represent third-party interests in conflict and order. The once-clear line drawn between self-help and governmental social control and between governmental and nongovernmental social control is fading.

Also encompassed in the idea of policing are two broad ways of formally organizing policing activities — those representing private or corporate interests, which are diverse and not directly under the purview of the state's agents, and those representing the public interest, which ostensibly act to control public spaces and relationships in the interest of the state.

This distinction between public and private policing, once clearly marking a well-understood conception of the division of labor within policing, has been blurred by practical developments and scholarly investigation in the last thirty years (Draper 1979, 163; Shearing 1992). Increasingly, the public-private division is seen as an analytic one, indicating nominal differences along several dimensions: policing emphasis and priorities, sources of pay, territorial responsibilities, accountability, and legal constraints, rather than concretely identifying interests or even degrees of moral opprobrium or rectitude.

❏ THE RISE OF POLICING

Policing is but one form of social control. All forms of social control, although they display consequences when seen as independent variables, are also dependent variables.[6] Similarly, all forms of policing use various strategies to both maintain compliance and increase their power. Policing, a formal mode of control, utilizes primarily the penal style when it appears, and reflects systematic variation in (prior extant) social norms.

It is possible to identify the conditions under which forms of policing arose (Radzinowicz 1948–66; Bayley 1975, 1979; Silver 1967; Miller 1977; Johnston 1992), and to note similarities across nations and over time. The emergence of policing forms, public or private, and their concrete institutional realization seem to be associated with a number of social processes. These include rapid social change, especially collective violence, explosions of dissent, questioning of governmental authority and its expansion, rapidly rising and falling status groups, symbolic disarray and reorganization, and emergent modes of protecting and transferring property and information (Draper 1979, ch. 2).

These perturbations in social order are not uncommon in modern democracies and can be located broadly in the early and late nineteenth century, in the mid-twentieth century, which saw a massive, worldwide depression and World War II, and in the present time. Periods of consolidation and integration appear to follow each period of reorganization. Arguably, the end of this century is witnessing similar upheavals and reorganization in policing, as seen in the reform movement called "community policing," in the growth of gated communities (Davis, 1992), and in the upheaval and downsizing, taking place in private security.

Private policing also emerged and grew under conflict conditions. It witnessed three periods of inception, consolidation and growth. It emerged in the mid-1850s in America with the invention of the alarm and with the widespread use of the stagecoach and the railroad and the need to protect mobile passengers and property, symbolized by the establishment of American Express, Pinkerton's (Morn 1992), Wells Fargo, and later, Brink's. These firms were established in a nine-year period between 1850 and 1859 (Johnston 1992, 20). A second period of growth was the period between the wars when unionization and miner's strikes threatened corporate interests. The most remarkable period has been the last twenty-five years, in which private security employees soon exceeded public employees by a ratio of 4 to 3, and private security lost its association with self-serving corporate violence, semilegal tactics, and greed (Nalla and Newman 1993, 15–33). Public policing has had uneven growth in America, with spurts of growth followed by job freezes, layoffs, pressures for retiring, and elastic budgets (Reaves 1996).

The balance between the forms of policing is historically determined, and as it changes, assessment of the value of the contributions can be made.

Dramaturgy and Dramas of Control

To consider policing and privatization one needs a framework. Because policing is linked to justice, morality, law, power, and authority, it plays a continuing part in the theater of modern life. This book views society as if it were a theater and the police as actors on the social stage. The police are the primary link between the state and citizens. What follows is cast in a dramaturgical-theatrical perspective and attempts to render policing as a kind of theater. We may envision two kinds of theater: one that shows a drama of regulation, ordering, and control and one that represents policing as the object of the mass media, as a form of entertainment offering visual orgies and spectacle.

The theatrical metaphor can be misleading if viewed as merely whimsical or as undermining the seriousness and consequentiality of policing. Acting takes place in a constraining material world within which meaning must be learned and negotiated. As one colleague of mine asked after a session on policing as communication: "Where are the bodies, the blood, the violence?" They must be held ever in mind. The drama of control entails death, suffering, emotional and social costs, and material and monetary costs, as well as epiphanies and moments of honor and dignity. These are unequally visited on the marginal, the poor, and the lower classes. The social costs borne by the marginal and the police-dependent and the costs of crime itself are in tension with the crude economics of "efficiency" used to assess the value and future directions of policing.

A dramaturgical perspective highlights the points of tension and ambiguities between concepts and actions, words and deeds, within the institutions of social control. Furthermore, it allows one to peer into the production of socially induced blindness, "institutional misrecognition" (Bourdieu 1977, 44) — the ways in which loyalty to institutions limits one's vision, choices, strategies, and tactics in everyday life. Both scholars and practitioners share these blind spots as well as an intense interest in the great drama of social integration and division, the theaters of control.

If society is a kind of big drama, played in a theater in which dramas are produced, tragedies are performed, and fates are displayed, and where grace, redemption, and salvation in all their forms are revealed, then one might think of types of policing (and the courts, corrections systems, probation, and parole) as producing little dramas of power with rather more limited resources, audiences, and consequentiality than the mighty dramas that periodically engage the public mind.

Periodically, there are police dramas — such as the beating of Rodney King, the trial of O. J. Simpson, the great Brink's robbery, and the clashes between the police and the miners in the 1984–85 British miners' strike, become media events and important social spectacles. More commonly, police engage in little dramas played on local stages to local audiences watching and listening, peering in using the media's eyes and ears. But these local dramas increasingly have the potential to become national and international media events.

Dramaturgical sociology sees social life metaphorically, as if it were theater. It studies the ways in which patterns of communication *selectively* sustain definitions of situations (a coded or schematic picture). This process of selective presentation constitutes drama. Actors — persons, groups, and organizations — perform using fronts (appearance, manner, and props) and settings (places in which behavior takes place) to convey realizations and idealizations to audiences. Through dramas, society and organizations imagine, constitute, and speak to themselves about themselves. Organizational dramas, especially "core dramas" and related narratives, shape and commit selves: they reveal the meanings of selves and collective actions. Through dramas, the self is embedded in social organization, and the line between the enacted self and the organization is a blurred line.

Celebrations of central sentiments and selves are core dramas, which integrate at least some selves into the organization. Consider one core drama, a military or police funeral: it serves to honor the dead, enhance social values, and renew the faith of the living in the continuity of order. Such dramas honor both the living and the dead, renew social attachments to the organization, restore morale and belief in one's roles and obligations, and enhance the loyal self. Of course, they mark the marginality of those who don't share the core values the organization displays.

Organizations act in the world on the basis of an orientation to the subjective order of authority with which actors comply. Organizations differentially encourage self-investment or attachment to organizational roles and self-affirming integration. In this context, policing actions can either inhibit or enhance loyalty.

Most of the routines of policing require teamwork and loyalty from participants, both performers and audience, who cooperate in creating, maintaining, and recreating a projected definition of the situation (Goffman 1959, 104), and in controlling access to any places that are bounded by barriers to perception (Goffman 1959, 107ff). Such a project implies a cooperative and tolerant attitude, or "tact," and trust, both within the team and on the part of audiences. If a plan of action for ensuring security does not co-opt the relevant audience and elevate its awareness of risks and assets, then it is not only a presentational failure, but it communicates the organization's capacity for self-governance.

Control is done and should be seen to be done. Symbolization of order, control, and contrasts between public and private displays and representations, create visible dramas. The drama of social control, how symbols and social relations are selectively marked (either suppressed or elevated in importance) by agents of control, and the resultant ordering, is central to my arguments. The appearance and symbolization of control compete with alternative social realities and material constraints.

Following the dramatic metaphor one step further, one can see that grand conceptions of private and public policing, such as those developed over the last seventeen years by Shearing and Stenning (1981, 1983, 1987; Shearing 1992), innovators in the field, explore and delimit the relationships between the structure of production and the little theater of policing. This is perhaps essential in order to delineate and distinguish the police from other forms and theaters or subsystems of social control (Reiss 1974).

It is perhaps fruitful now to examine social types of policing composed of analytically derived elements (Weber 1949). This typological approach will enable us to identify both similarities and differences in policing. It also outlines the analytic elements of policing as an ideal type that will be used to compare across types of policing. Simple distinctions derived from law, private interests, or foci (on prevention vs. punishment) appear to be overdrawn. The study of police organization, structure, strategies, and tactics broadens the focus and suggests that crises exist in both. Although the internal consequences vary, and the solutions debated are various, both are responding to the fragmentation and questioning of all forms of authority. The following section describes changes in modes of shared operation, organization, and function, pointing out that current modes of organization in policing blur easy distinctions and that many functions and strategies are either overlapping or in fact shared. The crisis in policing is discussed in two sections. "The Public-Private Dialectic" section is intended as an intellectual bridge between two organizational forms in crisis. It identifies eight dilemmas of "privatization." Competition and cooperation in the struggle over control of semipublic spaces (parks, malls, arenas, stadiums, and other stages for spectacles), are ongoing. This suggests that definitions distinguishing public and private policing on the basis of (roughly) territorial/spatial or public/private space are misleading. Chapter 6 discusses the emergence of new forms of competition and cooperation in policing, as well as the internal crises in both, and suggests that the future will show impacts of information technology, virtual organization, and transnational policing. How will the present dilemmas and contradictions in policing be played out in the next ten years? A brief conclusion, "Dilemmas and Contradictions," ends my part of the book.

❏ VARIATIONS IN POLICING

This section elaborates a definition of policing and identifies its "strategic ambiguities." It then outlines and discusses elements of policing. I argue for similarities in the political, functional, and symbolic functions of public and private policing and parallels in the shifting objects of police attention.

Ambiguities of Policing

Policing has a core or essential meaning: it is a formal mode of social control primarily utilizing the penal style (or punishment focused on the act). There are many forms of policing, using a mix of styles of control and strategies. All forms of policing involve third-party regulation or governance. That is, policing is a means to control: to inspect, evaluate, and respond to behavior on the basis of norms using a range of styles with the force of authority. The source of that authority varies.

Like all definitions, this highlights useful gaps or strategic ambiguities. These are "terms that clearly reveal the strategic spots where ambiguities necessarily arise" (Burke 1962, xx). Precision is but one aspect of definition, for vague, inconsistent, tautological definitions serve many political purposes. Definitions always contain multiple facets and reveal social attitudes and institutional contradictions. Recall that the drama of control means groups place selective emphasis via symbols upon facets of communication or messages intended for an audience. From a dramaturgical perspective, a definition seeks to uncover ironies and central paradoxes in a term — in this case, "policing." A number can be identified. Consider the following.

- Police control and coerce (investigate and control crime, produce order, monitor traffic) in the face of the vagaries of the human condition, regardless of the willingness of the citizens to comply. This raises the question of whether violence will be applied in the absence of compliance, but not when it will be applied, to and by whom, or in what amounts.
- Police provide essential violence in a society that publicly eschews it and claims Victorian standards as its measure of civility (Bittner 1970:17). Ironically, a police idea that originated in the grand and elevating notions of restraint and deterrence developed in the late eighteenth century by Jeremy Bentham, Edward Chadwick, and John Stuart Mill finds its fundamental grounding in to-be-avoided violence.

- To say that police "enforce the law" is misleading. Rarely do police directly invoke the law. Appeals to the law are useful — they mystify limited police powers, and elevate the risks of deviance, and justify actions. The law provides no prospective guidance concerning when it should be applied. The law is thus a resource, not the principal constraint on police conduct (Bittner 1970, chs. 5 and 6).
- The term "peace officer" as a synonym for "police" is an oxymoron, suggesting that the officer is peaceful and the task is peacemaking. Though its object may be peacemaking, the task is profoundly violent. Keeping the peace is the unexplicated background to the foreground of force and potential force.

These strategic ambiguities suggest that police and other politicians use dramaturgical work to sustain a nuanced edge between violence and control and order, and that much of this, selectively maintaining a working mandate, proceeds backstage and is unseen. Like all institutions, policing manages enduring social risks and maintains the appearance of control over the insolvable. The facade of order and control is always just that.

However, policing is not merely manipulating appearances. Public trust and confidence in the police in a democracy are essential. Nevertheless, the police claim an impossible mandate, like all professions, and must combine efficacy with ritual and myth and sustain high credibility. As individuals they must master the arts of team performance and impression management.

Social control refers broadly to the normative-evaluative dimension of social life and implies reaction to behavior with sanctions intended to shape, punish, or correct it in some fashion. Control implies extant and visible deviation from some standard or norm. Thus, though not all violations of norms are known or sanctioned, the police, governed by discretion, hold ready sanctions in the event they will have to intervene, as needed or called.

The police use several *styles of control* — *penal* (a focus on the act), *compensatory* (a focus on the consequences of the deviance), *conciliatory* (a focus on the relationship), and *therapeutic* (a focus on the person) — sometimes simultaneously in a graded fashion, sometimes only one (Black 1980). The penal and law enforcement style is used infrequently but is overly emphasized by researchers; the compensatory style is often used in handling juvenile offenses; conciliation remains a common style, for police remain, in spite of recent laws mandating arrest in domestic disputes, mediators and negotiators in domestic and neighbor disagreements. They would eschew this characterization perhaps, but they often counsel, advise, and support individuals in conflict situations.[7]

Although police focus has been on managing conflict or reacting to offenses, recent emphasis on problem solving and prevention has diminished the differences between public and private police. Police may attempt to (1) deter, (2) manage or react to (3) prevent incidents or problems, (4) minimize consequences through risk management, or (5) sanction the discovered wrongdoers. Any police-citizen encounter could involve any or all of the above.[9]

These strategies and tactics vary in degree and in the characteristic mix developed by agents and agencies. Given that most policing is dispatch-driven and reactive to information received, rather than based on proactive strategies or intelligence, police most often arrive after the fact of an incident and employ penal or management styles.

Territory is not a necessary feature of modern policing in spite of its nominal role in assignments and jurisdiction. Space is assigned and used variously across police agencies and within an agency. Specialized units may patrol an entire city or mall, and some units work only days, not territories. On uniformed patrol, police vehicles patrol and respond not only in their assigned areas but across the city, often patrol in other precincts, and provide backup informally in nearby jurisdictions. A major incident can bring units from three to five departments (if they can monitor one another's calls). Transnational policing, an emerging trend, shows that policing no longer has tight national, spatial, legal, or territorial limits. Cyberspace is now policed by many federal agents, including the FBI, and is a growing concern as a site for morals offenses.

Types of Policing

Weber argued that historical analysis is best accomplished by creating abstracted, exaggerated typifications of social actions and social units in order to compare their distinctive or defining elements (1949, 55). This suggests that a few elements that define policing should be identified and subtypes perhaps created from comparison of them. In this way, "self-help," policing based on self or narrow group interests, can be contrasted with private and public policing as social forms.

Elements of policing that cluster together can be identified. The first is the source of authority to intervene or react and ready justifications for this authority. The second is the basis (legal) for the obligation to act and, by extension, the persons to whom the police are accountable. The third is the interests served. Police are described as "disinterested": they act on behalf of some corporate entity in aid of maintaining order. The fourth is source and kind of payment and/or reward paid the police. In rational policing, salaries are linked to positions — or "offices," in Weber's terms — and often linked to management and budgeting practices. The fifth element is the nature of the training, recruitment, and equipment used. The sixth element is the role of the controller in the context of societal authority.

These six, taken together, constitute the elements of a mandate, or the scope of societal authority to act with impunity and be permitted mistakes (Hughes 1971).

Table 2.1 expands on these elements in its comparison of three types of policing — self-help, private policing, and public policing. These elements are arrayed against three broad types of social control. The last two are third-party forms of control, whereas self-help is direct personal and personalized involvement in a conflict. This means that relational distance between conflicting parties, although important in both, is more characteristic of self-help than of third-party interventions (Black 1980). Table 2.1 is not intended to suggest that policing "evolves" or "progresses" in some direction or to convey an invidious comparison; it is heuristic. The complex relations between public and private police are set in the context of democratic capitalism with market economies; and this force shapes organizational niches, strategies, and patterns of competition (Spitzer and Scull 1977). As these elements shift in importance or disappear, mandates change. Both public and private types of policing are now in a period of transformation of their mandates, but this is often confused with the objects, places, and people controlled.

Dynamic Aspects of Control

The three forms of policing share a concern for ordering and controlling, but the targets of control, the strategies and tactics used, and the laws that pattern control vary over time. Because the police mandate is constrained by the right to apply violence and the grounding norm of state authority (Bittner 1970; Kelsen 1961), some argue that the police are a conservative occupation that resists change and reform. The argument, which requires elaboration and specification, goes as follows.

The police are an archaic occupation. The core role expectation is the situational application of force, but this requires both strength and restraint. The police are linked symbolically with the medieval Christian tradition of knighthood, honor, and duty. They serve the state's higher espoused

TABLE 2.1 Comparisons of Self-Help, Private Policing, and Public Policing

Elements of Policing	Self-Help	Private Policing	Public Policing
Legal authority	Limited to self-defense	Limited to citizen powers in public places	Broad *de facto,* but limited in theory
Territory	Local (e.g., neighborhood)	Designated "private" by corporate boundaries	Public spaces within a jurisdiction
Obligation to act	Offense to personal familial interests, (e.g., honor)	Threat to corporate interests (usually as defined by top management)	Threat to the state and its interests or actual crimes
Domain of interests	Personal (revenge, self-help)	Private	Collective goods: public interest
Target group(s)	Offenders	Those in private space or threatening private interests	Citizens, especially lower classes, minorities, and youth ("the disorderly")
Rationale/ mandate	Collectively, none	Corporate charter, mission	Regulating *risk:* , prevent, deter manage, and control
Loyalty	To family name, history, tradition, gender	To corporation, especially, top management	To citizens and colleagues
Budgeting	None or informal	Highly volatile and political	Quite stable, traditional
Source of budget	N/A	Corporate budgets and emergency or contingency funds and contracts	City budget and grants, gifts and contracts
Training	None	Variable — mostly minimal	16 weeks+
Recruitment	None	Private. standards constrained by state and federal laws	Legal, written standards

TABLE 2.1 *(Continued)*

Elements of Policing	Self-Help	Private Policing	Public Policing
Arms	Various	Variable in distribution and type of weapon issued and carried	Variable — now widely 9mm semiautomatic as handgun and variety of other weapons (helicopters, tanks, submachine guns, etc.)
Key or core function	Restore sentiments — satisfying revenge—and establishing the worth of personal attachments	Protect interests, apply force (as Bittner 1970 defines)	Restrain and apply force per Bittner definition

principles and stated mottoes. Further, their attachment to force and honor places them outside the course of sectarian events. They are watchers, standing above the moral fray until and unless they define their role as requiring them to plunge into the secular world to (strike a moral balance) (as they read it), seek the just (as they see it), and produce a good (as they define it). Police blend the infrequent application of violence with an appreciation of its aberrant origins and quotidian character. For a patrol officer, the key to effectiveness is judgment and restraint, not applied violence.

This situational formulation rests on a slight misreading of the history of Anglo-American policing and restricts the definition of violence to concretely applied force. Thus, it ignores the importance of symbolic violence, violations of the social space of a person or group in the name of the state.

In Anglo-American society, individual police identify with the status quo and are asked to defend and protect it using democratically derived procedures. They defend the status quo as defined by the political elites and the law. When it changes, their obligations change. They are expected to act against their own class (Reiner 1978) or status interests in demonstrations and rallies. Sometimes ironically, since it involves controlling populations whose origins — similar class, and ethnic backgrounds — they share, police are actively engaged in dramatic marking and arranging of the vertical and horizontal order, and in defending, in a variety of ways, the status quo. The public police acted to protect workers in the miners' strike in Britain in 1984–85, functioning as did the Pinkertons during the miners' strikes in Ohio and Pennsylvania in the 1920s, the private strikebreakers hired by Henry Ford and Harry Bennett to break the emerging UAW led by the Reuther brothers, and community leaders and informal citizens' patrols in Watts in 1965. As agents of the state, police sustain the current hierarchy of legitimate interests and are bound publicly by the limits of public morality. The authority, legitimacy, and law are resources in replicating the present order.

Policing is a drama that expands into "big theater" or spectacles (Edelman 1988; P.K. Manning 1996) from the more sequestered "little theaters" (Foucault 1977, 113) in which it is normally featured. Theaters are of course stages, including actors, settings, scenes, and acts (Burke 1962, preface) that display and reproduce dominant and subordinate social orders. Representations of formal authority display conventional symbols and actions, as well as suppress other readings of authority. The sedimentation of good will and trust located in authority of course varies in time and by social segments, but it cumulates in *symbolic capital* (Bourdieu 1977, 6), or what is valued, exchanged, and sought in a society.

Social controllers interpose their "will" symbolically in exchanges between groups and thus redefine the meaning of symbolic action. This redefinition in turn may mean that by identifying with authority and the state, people fail to recognize their direct personal interests. The strategies of control create "lags" or temporal problematics in exchange. The discipline of the state is substituted for informal visible social control, and the experience, embodied and collectively, is changed.

These little and big theaters and dramas of policing serve to maintain the vertical order and the symbolic hierarchy of worth and have been dramatized by media variously in Anglo-American societies. Consider the following examples (P.K. Manning 1994c):

- The criminal law, among other legal sanctions and regulatory actions, is used by police to restrict the movements and activities of the poor and marginal and to protect property. It has been used also to control rising groups, as in the case of the English Factories Act (Carson 1970), to control social behavior, as by Prohibition (Gusfield 1966) and abortion regulations, and to restrain the lower classes from opportunities such as voting.

- As activities either decline in popularity or drift downward and are adopted by the lower classes, they are defined as criminal, and their perpetrators are subject to arrest and prosecution. This is revealed in a close analysis of changes in the control of rural English sports of hunting and bull and bear baiting. The move to raise taxes on tobacco, sue the tobacco manufacturers, and criminalize sales to juveniles arises from increases in use among the young of the middle class and the drift downward of the habit as educated people abandon smoking.

- As habits and lifestyles drift upward and gain respectability, they are redefined, decriminalized, or made legal, as seen recently in new tolerance for casino gambling, some drug use, and commercial sex.

- Certain "deviant" lifestyles are stigmatized and defined as criminal. Activities publicly associated with lower classes, native peoples, or immigrant pastimes and lifestyles, such as cockfighting, dog fights, and peyote use, are subject to criminal sanction.

- Space is regulated to maintain control of symbolically valued property and places. Changes in the uses and control of space marginalize certain powerless groups and place them at risk from public and private policing. The conflict over control of shopping malls illustrates conflicts of race and class, and increasing coalescence of public and private police to target and control visible minority youths in malls.

- Shared activities are differentially sanctioned. When leisure activities, are shared by middle and lower-middle classes, such as sport gambling, the middle-class form is legalized while the lower-class form(s) are made subject to the criminal sanction and police-initiated control.

- Lifestyle conflicts or "cultural wars" between cultural segments such as the fundamentalist Catholics and Protestants and more liberal or agnostic groups (e.g., conflicts over alcohol use and legal abortion) may stimulate movements to redefine some behavior or lifestyles as criminal.

- When the strategy used to control markets changes from eradication (a "war on drugs") to regulation (decriminalization of drug use) or vice versa, the targets of control also shift. In markets where eradication is thematic, the focus is on buyers and users, while in a regulated market, the focus is providers and distributors (Manning and Redlinger 1977).

- Dissent, such as flag burning, public demonstrations, and draft evasion, when carried out by members of the dominant coalition, is treated sub rosa and with discretion within the criminal justice system, while marginal groups are given the full benefit and force of the law.

- The visibility and size of deviant groups are always relevant considerations in control tactics, but with video surveillance, the lower classes are particularly subject to intrusive monitoring in semipublic spaces such as malls, train stations and airports, and sports events.
- In very large public spectacles, such as parades, massive sporting events, and especially international events like the Olympics, coalitions of public and private police cooperate and create a shared division of labor to order and patrol semipublic spaces and decide on sanctioning procedures and modalities.

In short, social change arises from the dialectic between class interests and control processes. While the content of the "threat" and "disorder" shifts, the form (criminal sanctioning) and direction of governmental social control or law continue to move downward. The fundamental ground is maintenance of the symbolic capital of the police, class control and political ordering. Only the definitions of phenomena and objects requiring control change. Both rising groups and the powerless are potential targets for control and regulation.

Since adherence to a rule, any rule, is itself the source of rewards, status, and self-esteem, as is the enforcement of such rules, the indirect value of compliance to the controlled and the controllers is retention of their own symbolic capital. Those on the political edges of society are denied access to both the material and symbolic resources of the society. Constantly changing control strategies, and coalitions of private and public police, create misrecognition by the powerless of their interests and in turn obscure police interests (Bourdieu 1977, 44).

Once it is seen that policing authority takes many forms and that it is intended to maintain control rather than to achieve an end, purpose, or normatively defined state (peace, order, tranquility, neighborhood pacification), it is clear that the drama of control has varied scripts, outcomes, strategies, and tactics. For example, Skogan and Harnett (1997, 6–9) refer to community policing as police work that leaves the development of tactics to the practitioners; it embeds the police in the community.

Policing in one respect is a flexible game of control using varying strategies and tactics and attending to shifting objects of control. This "gaming" metaphor is consistent with the cynical view of the patrol officer who sees the work as skillfully managing incidents caused by forces outside his or her control, repetitive and intrusive, enduring and in the nature of things. In this context, moral outrage is not only rare, it is exhausting, counterproductive, and illusory. Morality and expediency are combined in the craft-line practice of the patrol officer, even though such flexibility may facilitate net widening and the spread of social control (Cohen, 1985).

In short, the police respond to incidents they deem in need of control, but they do so through the perspective of corporate (social and collective) interests. This contrasts with Self-help, an attempt to right a wrong by direct *personal* intervention. What the police call crime is also a form of self-help-based social control (Black 1983).

Conclusions

It has been argued that definitions of police and policing must be placed in context, and elements and ideal types developed. Ideal types illustrate the dimensions along which policing varies. This typological exercise (table 1) sets the stage for an examination of the dialectic between public and private policing and their mutual concern with patrolling and maintaining moral boundaries, horizontal (status) and vertical (class) hierarchies of worth, and their own symbolic capital.

These changes create an air or ambience of vulnerability in both forms of policing. The public police, perhaps to a greater extent than other public sector institutions, such as social services, education, and the rest of the criminal justice system, are on the borderlines or crossroads of changing informal social controls and formal controls. These changes, redefining the police mandate and reorganizing functions — a consequence of the political economy — are complemented by a confusion and conflation of risk and uncertainty with a potentially negative outcome, crime and the fear of crime.

The next section considers the crisis in public policing, along with the market forces shaping it, the management trends and fads affecting internal organization, and some of the implications of the community policing movement. For example, the movement toward community policing, which in essence is an attempt to reduce social distance between the police and their publics, highlights the efforts of policing to redefine the team, team-work, the key audiences, their strategies and styles of control, and their interactional tactics.

❏ THE CRISIS IN AUTHORITY IN PUBLIC POLICING

There is a crisis, or reflective pause, in the world of public policing. It is the result of two primary forces: the market's impact on police reform and the rhetoric of rational management. The commodification or pricing of services based on market costs rather than as collective goods paid for and enjoyed by all, and the popular neoliberalism of police reformers, means that market standards are applied indiscriminately to human services. Even the notion of "services" has become a useful cliché covering everything from selling cigarettes ("tobacco services"), operating prisons, and giving traffic tickets to sex. The police reform movement's ideology is consistent with the low-tax antigovernment environment of public opinion in Europe and America. The rhetoric of economics features prominently in the police reform movement, because through advocating efficiency and "frictionless" transactions that satisfy "customers" and reduce social distance, the fantasy of instant responsiveness, of a serving police, rather than a distant, authoritative, and legalistic police, is imagined and sold to the public. The role of violence, coercion, and control is relegated rhetorically to mere shadows of past practices.

This section links rhetorical changes and market forces, transformations in the environment of urban policing, with police reform movements and points out the most salient consequences of associating police reform with economic language.

Changes in Policing since 1967

Important and consequential changes have occurred in American urban policing since the late sixties. These include alterations in police budgets, the pattern of public support for police, police involvement with the media, and the linkage of police command officers with reform movements. Other changes in urban policing are increases in the educational level of officers, changes in the sexual and ethnic composition of urban forces, presence of more legal standards constraining police practice, and the immediate presence and availability of new information technologies to the police.[9]

The police are losing their once-assumed monopoly of legitimate violence and now compete with self-help groups, private security firms, and the media for dominance in the drama of social control. Perhaps as a result, the language of economics and management is used to reconceptualize the police mandate. Consider these trends. Increasingly, the language of economics and management have penetrated the police literature and shape police training. Policing is called a service, and those they serve are injudiciously called customers, while shoppers in supermarkets are called guests assisted by associates. Marketing and image become more salient (Mawby 1997).

The first changes of note are economic. The infrastructure of cities has deteriorated even as city budgets have grown. The escalating costs of governance now exceed the willingness of taxpayers to meet them. The economic distress of cities is reflected in the elastic character of police budgets. As budgets shrink, the ratio of officers to citizens in urban areas has increased: there are in fact fewer officers per citizen in 1991 in urban areas than there were fifteen years ago.[10] It is not clear that monetary support for policing, when contrasted with that for other agencies funded by municipal budgets, has increased proportionately in this century (Bordua and Haurek 1971). The growth in policing is in small towns, in suburbia and the urban-rural fringe, not in large cities (Weisheit, Falcone, and Wells 1993). Many police forces face serious budget cuts, layoffs, and cycles of hiring — blitzes and chilling freezes. These oscillations surely affect morale and the degree of loyalty officers show to command personnel, certainly create chaos, and may well increase turnover.

A second change is in public support for police. Variations in the degree of public support for police and policing are difficult to chart. Support in urban areas measured by public opinion polls has declined while fear of violent crime and drug related crimes has increased generally (Warr 1995).

A third change is the nagging remnants of the last seventy plus years of crime-focused policing, reborn under misleading labels like "zero tolerance" (Kelling and Coles 1997). In spite of research demonstrating that the police provide a variety of functions, and that there is virtually no systematic statistical relationship between police strength and official crime statistics, the police continue to claim that they are primarily, if not exclusively, "crime fighters." This is patently true of patrol officers who are on the front line daily.

Even some academic writers argue that the "core mission of the police is to control crime. No one disputes this" (Moore, Trojanowicz, and Kelling 1988). Nevertheless, many do dispute this (Goldstein 1990; P.K. Manning 1997), and such a flat statement begs the question of the extent to which this is practical or even possible, given the other factors that pattern and alter criminal conduct, crime rates, and clearance rates. The police can manipulate crime statistics and perhaps create periodic troughs in official statistics by crime attack and zero tolerance tactics, but independent measures suggest that these dips in the official rates are temporary and ephemeral and shaped by many other factors. The dark figure of unreported crime always exceeds the crime known or reported. The experience of the last thirty years suggests that even brief drops in the official crime figures signal imminent new rises.[11]

Zero tolerance campaigns signal coalescing of private and public police in action (Kelling and Coles 1997, ch. 6) as well as the retrograde side of crime-focused and crime-suppression tactics that pander to the middle-class concerns about fear of crime and urban chaos or disorder and play to the fantasy that control of urban streets can be taken back by the police as if the police or any group were ever in control of public spaces.

A fourth change is the increase in the workload of police officers, especially in large cities. Granted that the amount of notional free time driving around and patrolling remains substantial (Bayley, 1994:40–44), other social forces may well contribute to driving up the patrol officer's workload. The number of crimes and incidents processed, even when balanced against population rise, is increasing. The rise in reported crime is not balanced by increases in the size of urban forces. Police are assigned more direct functions, such as problem solving or community policing (whatever it refers to), but are given no additional relief from radio-dispatched calls.

A fifth change is the role of the media in social control. In this dynamic relationship between crime, fear of crime, and public support, the media are playing a more apparent role (Altheide 1992, 1997). The media, with police cooperation, play on crime news and amplify public fear (see Ericson 1989, 1991; Warr 1995). In addition, the media have glamorized police leadership. That is, they have sanctified the myth of command and control and mystified the nature of police practices, especially the use of violence.[12] The rhetoric of community policing appeals to the media and the middle classes and obscures the core of violence expected and required of the police. The police, in turn, have developed sophisticated media skills which enable them to shape public perceptions of crime. As the experience of Commissioner Bratton's claims for crime reduction in New York in 1995 illustrate, the police and the media shape the social reality of crime. Television produces crime-simulation shows combining news film of events with reenactments, voice-over narration by actors and actresses, and grainy video filming with hand-held cameras intended to simulate reality. In addition, shows such as *Cops* screen well-filmed and engaging films of actual stops and raids. For the modern citizen in a large city, media reality is interdigitated with personal experience, simulations of events, feature films, the news, and on-the-spot videos—such as those of the Rodney King beating in March 1991 in Los Angeles and the Joanne Was beating in Detroit in August 1991.[13] A new social construction of the meaning of crime and social control is emerging.[14]

A sixth change is the police reform movement that has arisen and flourished since the Police Foundation was funded by the Ford Foundation in the late sixties. This movement now features police leaders and re-searchers in organizations like the Police Executive Research Forum, the Police Foundation, the National Institutes of Justice, the International Asso-ciation of Chiefs of Police, and the National Council of Mayors. The foci of police reform are many, but the most visible vehicle is called "community policing." Its vague status is of course a source of its political appeal. Community policing has had a wide, if not deep, impact on the rhetoric of policing in virtually every town in America (Mastrofski 1988), but such claims do not entail actual changes in organization, practices, attitudes, tactics, or functioning programs. The rhetoric, above all, indicates the wish of the police to reinvent big-city politics, restore their mandate, and reduce social distance with some of the publics they regulate.

A seventh change is that modern-day police, especially at the com-mand level, are more educated and reflective than the officers of thirty years ago. The rise in their educational level in part reflects the increase in education in society as a whole, and in part is the result of massive financial support given to officers to pay for higher education by the Law Enforce-ment Assistance Administration in the seventies (Mastrofski 1990: Sherman and the National Advisory Commission on Higher Education for Police Officers 1978). It is not clear what this change in educational level signifies for police practice or the quality of life in large American cities, but it has altered union-management negotiations about pay and conditions of work. It may, in due course, also change other practices, such as recruitment, promotion, evaluation, and supervision. Police officers with degrees in sociology, criminal justice, psychology, and political science, now hear themselves talking to one another and see themselves regularly on televi-sion. They confer and debate with academics in conferences, meetings, and bars; they present scholarly papers and write books. Many have have read the works of Bittner, Skolnick, O. W. Wilson, J. Q. Wilson, Reiss, and Rubinstein of the first generation (1962–1972) some of the second genera-tion of writers, (1972–present) and the fictions and semifictions of Joseph Wambaugh, Mark Baker, and others. Some officers with advanced degrees have taught or are teaching in criminal justice programs.

An eighth change is the composition of urban forces. Once a white male occupation, policing has diversified. In 1972, women made up 4.2 percent of police officers serving in urban departments in population areas above 50,000; by late 1988 this figure had increased to 8.8 percent. (Martin 1990). The percentage of African American and other minority groups in the same size departments is difficult to determine but is probably increasing, especially in very large cities (Mastrofski 1990, 20). Addition of non-officer staff increases apace, rising from 16.5 to 20.4 percent of police departmental personnel between 1976 and 1986 (Mastrofski 1990, 21).

A ninth change is the growth of legalism and fear of legal repercussions of police actions. Constraints upon police practice imposed by criminal and civil law have grown in importance. The *Miranda, Escobedo,* and *Mapp* decisions, and recent cases of the Supreme Court that make admissible coerced confessions and evidence seized in illegal searches, bear on procedural aspects of criminal law and continue to shape policing (del Carmen 1991). Once protected from civil suits, police are now liable. Negotiated out-of-court settlements are now a major source of expenditures in large cities (Mastrofski 1990). Civil liability may be shaping policing by increasing the perceived costs of violence to the department and the officer(s) involved.

A tenth change is the introduction of new information technologies such as computer-assisted dispatch and expanded, legally mandated 911 systems; management information systems; and computerized record keeping. The interiors of police cars have changed: they now contains cellular phones (both departmental and personal phones) mobile digital terminals, and sophisticated high-frequency radios, and officers may carry pagers. These promise to erode the traditional authority of first-line supervisors and police command. They may also significantly alter the role structure and distribution of skills in police departments (P.K. Manning 1992). A very powerful potential resides in information technologies now diffusing from large city to smaller urban departments, and the budgets of suburban departments mean that they have better and more up-to-date equipment than impoverished cities like Detroit. It is not clear that radio-dispatched 911 policing has "failed" (Kelling and Coles 1997, 89–107). Community policing has been added to this core workload in many communities.[15]

An eleventh change is in rhetoric as well as reality. The police are now viewed by some observers as businesses rather than humane, public service agencies with obligations to justice, fairness, legality, and civility. One indication of this is the popularity of stilted business management jargon now used to describe policing. Police chiefs are seen as analogous to CEOs, managing businesses and taking risks within a market context. They position their organizations for market shares, create lean and mean organizations do not tolerate indolence (Kelling and Coles, 1997, 144–145), and actively "run" the organization. Accreditation and continuing education seminars are offered on "Advanced Management for Law Enforcement Executives" (by the Southwestern Law Enforcement Institute, Richardson, Texas) and on "Law Enforcement Management" (by the Law Enforcement Institute and Sam Houston State University).

As noted above, the management focus in policing is not unrelated to trends revealing a deterioration in the police monopoly of violence (Bittner 1990). No longer a quasi-monopoly, the public police compete with private security firms and community action groups who use violence, and the media who simulate it, for legitimate, violent social control. Furthermore, the number of handguns (70 million, rising at about 1.5 to 2 million a year, or about one per every four households, Kleck 1991, table 2.1) continues to increase, and the police — local, state, and federal — have escalated the firepower contest by arming themselves with semiautomatic 9mm weapons.

Consequences of the Changes

There are several important consequences of these changes. The traditional bases of the police mandate, commitment to maintaining the collective good, serving with honor and loyalty, and observing tradition, are being modified (see Bordua and Reiss 1966). These bases are often in conflict with rational-legal control and with pragmatic concerns such as avoiding legal liabilities and civil suits and maintaining an "efficient operation." They are also in conflict with businesslike accounting procedures and tight budgetary constraints. Market efficiency is a never-ending mythical quest that contrasts with the limited, constrained, moderate mission of democratic policing. Is it true that the public requires efficient crime control at the cost of civil liberties, privacy, freedom of choice, and the like? Policing, depicted in economic discourse, is being incorporated into the political economy of capitalism. Its traditional, quasi-sacred status as a calling, an occupation insulated from the demands and exigencies of the market, is fast being eroded. It is now less "an occupationally organized community that sets itself apart" (Bordua and Reiss 1966, 68). The distinctive mode of organizing policing bureaucratically to reduce the claims of other loyalties, such as the market, ethnic communities, and family, is challenged by a market orientation to policing (Bordua and Reiss 1966, 68). The degree of competition with other forms of social control—namely, self-help (Black 1983) and private security — is increasing. A more pragmatic, businesslike form of policing that competes to win a market share risks its prestige, legally legitimated monopoly on violence, and stable funding. The effects of market competition, like deregulation, have yet to be fully envisioned.

These last developments possess a historical background worthy of a brief review. How did the present model of policing emerge?

Reform: Historical Background

It should be recalled that the origins of Anglo-American policing as a social institution are to be found in England in the mid-eighteenth century (Hart 1951, 1956; Silver 1967; Miller 1977; Critchley 1978; Emsley 1996). Public police arose because private and voluntary means for patrol and the protection of the capital were inadequate; they augmented but did not replace the myriad of private forces in London. Conversely, the later flowering of the private police in the United Kingdom and the United States occurred after a official police mandate had been claimed.

Tensions between public and private authority remain in American society. They are illustrated by the current emphasis on market controls and periodic attempts to reform the American police. In the mid-twentieth century, reform meant political reform. The present appeal to market forces for reform is an analogue of deregulation. It may reduce civic control over police command and police accountability.

American police reformers of the twenties and thirties, such as Harry Emerson Fosdick, Leonard Fuld, August Vollmer, and Bruce Smith, were trained as lawyers and public administrators (Stead 1977). The aims of police reform in that era appear to be the following.

These reformers aimed to isolate and protect policing from the corrupting forces of urban, ethnically based machine politics. They also sought to ensure that departments recruited, trained, and supervised officers with a commitment to the organization above ethnic, religious, and political (often territorially based) loyalties (Bordua 1966). They sought to develop a version of "scientific policing" based on applied technology, the crime lab, the radio, and the automobile. Vollmer and O. W. Wilson, in particular, sought to understand the causes of and modes of prevention and control of crime and connected the police mandate with the idea of active, effective, and scientifically based crime control. Reformers sought education of police command personnel to reflect developments in modern public administration. The aim of this important reform was to enhance the prestige, political power, and authority of police organizations.[16]

These coherent themes constituted the basis for policing reform, but as Reppetto (1978) shows convincingly, regional and local forces shaped policing in America and still do. Any sweeping generalization should be tempered with caution. Clearly, the intellectual founders sought to develop a new police mandate. It is clear, however, that the political processes and traditions of American cities shaped this reform movement and gave it local color and texture (Lane 1967; Fogelson 1977; Reppetto 1978; Monkonnen 1992).

The mandate, or underlying rationale for police authority, would be based on a strong and centralized command and rational legal authority. Guided by bureaucratic rules and applied science, professional policing would be legitimated in American cities (Wilson 1963). The key role in the changes played by forensic and social sciences, the two-way radio, the automobile, and the telephone cannot be underestimated. These shaped and were shaped by the police strategies that emerged. A number of developments have shaped police reform since this period.

Police administration is first concerned with discipline and control of officers and is means-oriented (Goldstein 1990, 15). Concern with command and control of officers rather than with crime control or political efficacy always threatened. Because a scientific mandate required command, control and direction of officers, attention shifted subtly, as noted in the work and writings of O. W. Wilson, to questions of internal control, to efficiency, and to applying the wisdom of public administration to governance of police departments. Policing would not just be a job but would be transformed into a quasi-scientific management position based on "police administration" and scientific crime control (see Carte and Carte 1977).

Police research became an aspect of police reform in the late sixties. The idea that research would guide and transform policing had great credence in academic circles following the publication of the Report of the President's Crime Commission (1967). William Westley's dissertation (1970), written in 1950, posed paradigmatic questions about the sources and role of secrecy, prejudice, and violence in policing. Westley noted police dislike of homosexuals and blacks and described the roots of their hatred and the rationalizations for violence directed to them. He pointed out the contradiction between police officers' violence toward minorities and their commitment to fair law enforcement. Jerome Skolnick (1966) argued that discipline, uniformity, and control themes fit uneasily with protection of the freedoms of a democratic society. The rule of law and street justice, "justice without trial," were in conflict. Skolnick appeared to put confidence in legal reforms and constraints.

The President's Crime Commission contracted for field studies of policing in three metropolitan areas (Chicago, Boston, and Washington,

D.C.) and set the standard for qualitative work for thirty years (Reiss 1971) The work of James Q. Wilson bridged the reformer's interests and those of social researchers. His now classic *Varieties of Police Behavior* (1968) insightfully noted that styles of policing were somehow shaped by the local "political culture." However, he argued that police administrators had turned inward, seeking to avoid mistakes, public embarrassment, and scandal. Little effort was made to develop long-term plans.

With the possible exception of Wilson's work, research on policing did not examine management, or command. Bordua and Reiss observed twenty-five years ago, in a still valid statement, "To our knowledge, there is no detailed empirical description of command processes in a police department" (1966, 68). Although Brown (1981) studied the impact on the street of different policies and administrative styles, he provided no context within which such policies were interpreted or understood. How such policies were actually implemented remains unclear.[17]

The late seventies saw a tighter focus on specialized policing, the rationalizing of police practices, and the counterpoint of critiques of these notions (Ericson 1981, 1982; P. K. Manning 1979). The language of productivity or efficiency was not employed until the early seventies, when it was featured as a means to reform felony arrest processing (Forst et al. 1976), detective work (Eck 1983), and police communications (Hough 1980a, 1980b; P. K. Manning 1988). Synthetic books such as Goldstein's (1977) disseminated research findings and critique in a clear and readable fashion to academics and practitioners.

Police administrators now participate in the dialogue of postindustrial society using the language of the policy sciences and economics to describe policing. They are subject to and aware of their own reflexive actions and discourse. The current rhetoric of choice includes service and public administration, community policing, zero tolerance, and managerial strategies and profit making.

These changes in policing, especially the metaphoric turn that conceives of policing as an economic institution, are part of the overall movement toward privatization of control, reduction of governmental supervision in favor of the market and private governments, and the use of the media to substitute symbolic imagery for direct, personal, and violent authority.

❏ THE MANAGEMENT CRISIS IN PUBLIC POLICING

This section outlines a rhetoric popular in public forces, a management philosophy — Total Quality Management (TQM) — and some of its attendant dilemmas. An analysis of economic imagery in policing is illuminating because public perceptions of organizations constrain strategies and choices and employees' loyalty. TQM is something of a synecdoche for economic reform in public administration and must be seen in the context of the police mandate. The extended analysis of TQM is used as a shorthand for simplistic solutions to policing and is not a rejection of economic analyses generally or of the need for police reform.

Imagery

Policing, like all organizations, relies on audiences and organizational performers who trust, credit, and internalize the imagery by which it defines itself and who accept both the mystification and the reality of the institutional mandate. Insofar as participants are committed to an organization, they tend to overvalue their own organization when compared with others. This halo effect has valuable positive consequences for morale, governance, performance, and external relations.

The police use ideology and myth to sustain their authority and to decouple their performances from their resources, budgets, and material assets (Meyer and Rowan 1977; Crank 1994; 1998; P. K. Manning 1997). Problems arise, however, when ideologically driven imagery outstrips established institutional functioning. There are material limits on symbolic claims and rhetoric such as crime control, zero tolerance, the "war on drugs" and other inflated self-serving claims. Furthermore, external audiences may tire of slogans and require evaluation or review. Police are questioning their mandate and seeking new validation and justification for their traditional functions.

An organization like public policing, now losing authority and witnessing the contraction of its mandate, reflects a struggle of imageries — several being proposed as part of reform movements. These include the paramilitary imagery, the public service community policing imagery, and the economic image. Policing as "risk management" is a recently coined image (Ericson and Haggerty 1997). Each has features that facilitate public compliance and trust and those that remain hidden or suppressed by rhetoric and image making.

Policing has long battled the paramilitary imagery developed in part to produce the semblance of managerial control over lower participants. This imagery of tight control, supervision, and swift punishment, as in the nineteenth century in England, has ideological force with citizens, managers, and politicians who fear police violence, deviance, and corruption.

The Police "Business"

Let us consider the case for conceiving of public policing as an economic, or corporate, activity. In 1988, Mark Moore, an economist, and the late Robert Trojanowicz, a professor of criminal justice, published "Corporate Strategies for Policing." Widely distributed by the U.S. Department of Justice and Harvard University's Kennedy School, it explicitly applies the corporate metaphor and management language to policing.

Policing is discussed as an expensive "service" (costing the taxpayers an estimated 20 billion dollars a year in 1988; it may have doubled by 1998). These monetary resources are "redeployed" with authority (pp. 1–2) using a "corporate strategy." Corporate strategy, a term borrowed from the private sector, refers to

> the principal financial and social goals the organization will pursue, and the principal products, technologies and production processes on which it will rely to achieve its goals. It also defines how the organization will relate to its employees and to its other constituencies such as shareholders, creditors, suppliers and customers. In short, a corporate strategy seeks to define for the organization how the organization will pursue values and the sort of an organization it will be. (p. 2, citing Andrews, 1980)

Policing is analyzed using the concept of corporate strategy. Policing, like other service industries, is viewed as occupying a market niche and competing through strategic means to maintain it (Moore and Trojanowicz 1988). The corporate strategy of the American police in the past fifty years, according to Moore and Trojanowicz, has been "professional crime fighting." It is based on centralization of command and control and communications, sharpened focus on crime control (p. 5) and substantial investment in modern technology and training. This strategy, in their view, is now exhausted and outmoded. They suggest a new corporate strategy and discuss new facets or modes of strategy such as "problem solving policing," "strategic (or proactive) policing," and "community policing." They argue for expanding the mission of the police using a combination of problem solving as a technique, a focusing on dangerous offenders, and fear reduction programs (p. 10). They note a tension between what they advocate, decentralized problem solving, a geographic definition of problems and close community interactions, and the previously emphasized administrative centralization, specialization, and independence from communities. They advocate a corporate shift into "professional, strategic, community problem-solving policing" (p. 14).

The Moore and Trojanowicz paper, and Moore's later book (1995), outlines a new rhetorical strategy for policing. It implies competition for resources which the police subsequently distribute, mobilization of those resources in a competitive market, and concern for demonstably successful market strategies. The previous strategies will be (or should be) replaced because they have failed in the marketplace. The police mission should be justified by maintaining a market niche and ensuring social profitability or value-added practices.

This contrast with previous visions of police reform, although they did claim efficiency as the result of scientific analysis of crime, information technology, and militaristic discipline. It also departs from institutional economic views of policing. Rather than seeing policing dispensing a "collective good" (Samuelson 1954; Feeley 1970) to which all must contribute and from which each gains, the new language sees it as a competitive, services-producing organization that must show a social profit and produce, advertise, package, market, and distribute its services to customers. The tension between providing collective goods and market competitiveness is mediated by the notion that satisfaction, indicating quality, creates value (Moore 1995; 53).

The economistic metaphor for policing and police reform has emerged since the early eighties and is consistent with the economic philosophy of the Reagan-Bush years. It conceptualizes policing in terms of supply and demand and in market-competitive terms. Economic, market-based imagery fits the current emphasis on efficient, low-cost, market-driven organizations, well managed and strategically positioned. The police are less vulnerable to ideological trends and fads, image making, and marketing because of their traditional connections with duty, service, honor, and violence, and their direct links to governance, local public administration, and budgeting. Whether their actual functions and the costs of policing are changing is another unanswered question. It not surprising in an era of high capitalism and rationalized greed that imagery and reality converge to portray all human services as unexplored pockets of profit.

The economic imagery that views policing as an imperfectly managed or even failed business has a seductive appeal for reformers. Clearly, the consequences of adopting this new economic imagery are complex and differ among police departments according to size, mission, and age. To review, this vision includes several features. Economic rhetoric — which caricatures public and private organizations as governed by a market and competing for a market share, subject to inexorable market mechanisms that reward efficiency, performance, and effectiveness; produce goods and services that can be compared strictly using a monetary metric; and have outputs, reward structures, and incentives that are universal, comparable, and measurable — has penetrated public sector organizations. Even the notion of "collective or public goods," to which all contribute and from which all benefit, has been reduced to a positive externality frequently passed on to the public sector by private corporations. Economistic thinking is now reshaping the infrastructure of evaluation, supervision, and reward throughout the "private sector": in universities, government, and governmental agencies such as the police, social services, and corrections.

Variants of economic imagery are found in appeals for total quality management (to reduce costs), continuing education and accreditation (to reduce liability and civil suits), and new information technologies (to reduce pass-through costs and increase output). All are couched in the language of the market, advance current managerial ideologies, and serve to constrain and bureaucratically manage the good people do for one another.

One consequence of the scientific management reform movement was to isolate officers in cars, reduce contact and interaction with the public, and contain corruption (Reiss 1992b). In time, policing became much more legalistic and shaped by court rulings, even while maintaining discretion and secrecy. Policing, stripped of its influence as a source of patronage, lost political power within local government. Reform ironically elevated the power of police unions and focused issues on the conditions of work because unions became the only viable form of collective opposition to command and control ideologies. Crime fighting became a managerial priority, while public contact, service, and providing comfort to the weak, helpless, and exploited did not. The police are challenged now to broaden their services while faced with rising costs and relatively reduced budgets and personnel.

Generally, new imagery is shaped and diffuses from the top, usually adopted or borrowed from other sources, and thus generally indicates managerial power. The police are affected by broad trends in American management and by the erosion of public sector autonomy and authority generally. For example, interest in TQM arises in part from the enthusiastic endorsement of budget and planning officers and City managers acting through their professional associations because control of police and police budgets is typically problematic and resisted by the police. Moreover, pressures for changes in police management are amplified by the current anti-intellectual populism (and an antigovernment congress) that support privatization of institutional functions and advocates market solutions and mechanisms to ameliorate social problems, bureaucractic stagnation, and ossification.

Arguments for TQM in Policing

The argument for TQM has apparent validity and appeal.[18] It is presented typically in a rather slick fashion in books, and the key concepts take their meaning from context, shift in meaning over time, and are often borrowed uncritically from the closed-system logic of economists. Let us first consider the broad assertions made and then examine their utility in policing.

TQM is said to produce results in industry by empowering employees insofar as mutual performance goals are negotiated with management. This serves to increase performance and so reduce transaction or pass-through costs. The consequence of these changes is seen indirectly in increased profit.

Such management is said also to encourage, or even perhaps require, more ethical supervision. It rejects a "blame and shame" mode that focuses on punishment of rule breaking and strives for mutually negotiated accountability and work-process analysis combined with ongoing feedback, evolution, and correction of mistakes. Instead of enduring unexpected and perhaps capricious managerial intervention after the completion of a "production sequence," workers are meant to internalize and "buy into" shared standards for evaluating the quality of work applied throughout the production process.

TQM is a means to transform organizations, making them at once more service-oriented and attentive to customer demands and needs, and eventually to precipitate customer-based modes of evaluation of products and services.

TQM is said to induce or bring about increased efficiency. It reduces the need for immediate work supervisors, since quality control is built into workers' values and the structure of the work of production; it reduces worker opposition to supervision because workers accept and internalize the nature of work processes and accountability; and it reduces time wasted on irrelevant tasks and reduces occupational deviance and lost worker time.

Arguably, it increases employee morale by integrating employees into managerial decisions and giving them a stake in the company (through stock options or profit sharing). On the other hand, material rewards are made less significant than symbolic ones, "stakes," and internal commitments to quality work will increase long-term worker satisfaction (see Hodson 1996).

Finally, TQM claims that it increases managerial flexibility. Because the "avoidance" or "shame and blame" culture (based on fear of punishment for mistakes) does not develop, and union strength may be undercut (a value from this managerial perspective) by workers' acceptance of TQM, cooperation replaces conflict.

Arguments against TQM in Policing

The economic metaphor embodied in the language of TQM when applied to people work is profoundly misleading. The question of efficiency applies the language of nineteenth-century economics to government service and draws on older time-and-motion approaches. Policing seems singularly maladapted to management changes based on TQM. There are several primary reasons for this, some of which have been mentioned in previous chapters.

I shall try to summarize the primary arguments. Policing does not "produce" a product. The "services" provided by policing are fundamentally subject to conflict and dispute and are collective goods (Samuelson 1954). The contributions of policing to civil society cannot be measured easily, demarcated narrowly, or reduced to a monetary metric because much of what they do is symbolic, representing other things such as social integration, community well-being, and a sense of propriety and security. At the same time police represent both the best and worst in society. On the one hand, they embody what is immoral, wrong, and outside the boundaries of acceptable conduct. On the other, they represent more indirectly the state, morality, and standards of civility and decency by which we judge ourselves. At best, they serve collective interests — the ones people find difficult to precisely define or express (though they know that these interests do not include exploiting the weak and the marginal to make a profit) — and at worst, its dark side.

The sacred and mysterious quality that attaches to policing endures because it is, metaphorically at least, a kind of service, even a gift that society employs to simulate and stimulate the best in citizens on behalf of others. Policing, even though it is seen as violent and a force fighting evil, also sustains moral values indirectly. The means used are pragmatic, not based on general moral or ethical principles. Economic values and moral values, as the works of Friedman and others show, are not necessarily contradictory in a democracy. However, if economic terms are used out of context, absent the political and social values that undergird our institutions, they erode the basic institutional contract. This contract is the reduction and mitigation of human risks and losses. This is the moral web in which we are entangled and by which we are sustained. Efficiency may well be in tension with other values such as equality of service or civil liberties.

Policing functions were converted from private to public functions in the Anglo-American world precisely because private police represented corrupt and violet actions, not to speak of desuetude and incompetence. At present, policing is "people work," and the primary police "technology" is language and speech — persuasion, guile, and lies, and ultimately, perhaps, threats and applied force. In this respect, the fundamental resource of police is public trust, and their obligation is to nurture and sustain it. Without trust and compliance, they must resort to force or unmitigated fraud. With this mandate, and in part because they deal with the unexpected, uneven, unpredictable, and diverse events dispersed over time and space and varying in scope, duration, and consequence, their mistakes are tolerated. They are a reserve force, retaining and nurturing "slack resources" (Thompson 1967), those held in abeyance for allocation to matters that arise. These personnel, weapons, tools, and reciprocal mutual aid obligations binding them to other agencies are built into the structure and process of policing. To trim (or add to) police resources on the basis of a hypothecated ideal level would fly in the face of all reasonable experience with hazards, terror, riots, fires, civil disturbance, and rebellion. These are seen as matters which if left alone could escalate and become even more vexatious and dangerous (Bittner 1990).

Policing is in many ways a tolerant, restrained craft which rewards moderation and discretion and overlooks many violations because democratic societies in principle expect tolerance and discretion rather than full enforcement of laws; they want a balance between humanity and civil liberties. The recent emphasis on community policing combined with intense crime-control policing ("zero-tolerance" tactics) and high arrest rates is but another policing paradox. Nevertheless, policing is about violence, its application, avoidance, skillful management, and incisive use; this is an unpopular public function and thus plans for its use in disasters, riots, massive uprisings, and public disorder are kept concealed, and are seldom discussed openly in public. Violence is revealed sporadically when high-speed chases kill innocent drivers or pedestrians, when the unharmed are shot, when beating and other forms of violence exceed community tolerance. The central and core function is locally judged, and notions and standards for measuring excessive force are mercurial.

There is an important question about the use of incentives to alter police behavior on the ground. An inspectorial bureaucracy like the police empowers the lower participants. They can control *praxis,* the level and kind of work done, and generally do. Thus, it is not surprising that patrol officers, or lower participants, remain loyal to the job and to economic rewards, not to fashionable rhetoric, nascent imagery, and shifting managerial ideologies. The tripartite police occupational culture, divided into command, middle management and lower participants (sergeants and patrol officers), means that the social bases of self-investment differ. The appearance of a new rhetoric in connection with police reform suggests, as it has since unions entered policing, a struggle between top command — management — and middle management (sergeants and lieutenants) and between middle management and the patrol officers.

The grand and elevated portrait I have painted above is not meant to diminish the violence, misplaced energies, and corruption of policing but to set its mission and values in light of broad standards of civic conduct.

Ironies of Applying TQM in Policing

This review of TQM suggests that it should be now viewed specifically in the police context. It advances a number of specific claims consistent with the views of those who have urged more "democratic" police management (Guyot 1991; Angell 1971). No research has established through close evaluation the advantages or disadvantages of adopting TQM in a police department, so one can only speculate. Let us consider some of the ironies of applying TQM to policing in the order discussed above.

TQM is designed to empower the worker, by reducing arbitrary managerial supervision and engendering mutual trust. The discretion of patrol officers who control "input" — information, prisoners, paper, and evidence — stands almost invisible and largely outside direct managerial authority. The values of the lower participants in patrol surround job control, original authority to act in the name of the state, and loyalty to one's colleagues. Reducing costs and increasing profits or even output has different meaning to subsegments of the patrol world (Walsh 1985). Most officers to not seek rank promotion. Some officers do seek rank promotion, time off, or overtime and related income, and some avoid work generally. The unity of this segment is based on opposition to managerial supervision and control, not loyalty to a common culture. Because police work is fundamentally uncertain, standards for judging it are clinical "You had to be there," a guiding idea, fact. Interventions by supervisors are (reduces) viewed as unwanted, capricious, and counter-productive.

The oppositional culture that develops around the lower participant's life interests has always been problematic for command officers (P.K. Manning 1997; ch. 6). The working officer's culture operates in effect to loosely couple managerial schemes, visions, and plans, intended to guide officers dealing with human misery and despair. It insulates the officer from bureaucratic rules on the one hand and from the publics on the other; provides the necessary cushion that permits slack to be mobilized, and enables situationally sound, shrewd, creative, and well-crafted responses to complex problems.

Perhaps TQM, which shifts emphasis from production to the process of producing, moves attention from the end to the means. Profits or costs deflect energies from concerns with quality, service, and durability, or from the means of production. Police have never been oriented to ends but rather more to means and to indexes of discipline, control, and supervision of the lower participants (Goldstein 1990, 15). The process of policing is the product and correctly the focus of management. The primary concern of command officers is not global aims: crime control, service, or order maintenance; it is the day-to-day activities of the patrol officer. Perhaps policing is more about the process of ordering than about particular and immediate ends.

TQM intends to increase responsiveness to the "customer," is a misleading and insidious term. The police are not universally popular — they keep a jail, arrest people, apply violence, write tickets, and surveil, control, and manage citizens' conduct. They are at the center of social conflicts. The role implies conflict and conflict resolution. The police officer does not serve individual citizens or seek to please them; the officer serves the public interest as the state and its political officers define it. This role is supported by law, public morality, and tradition. To reduce officers' functions to providing public service, even defined as a source of conflict, is to make a mockery of the work and the traditional mission of policing in a democratic society. Since the middle classes and above are typically seen more in the victim than in the offender role, responsiveness to the customer will hold within it a potential for producing increases in class inequalities, rationing of service to the more powerful and conventionally worthy, in order to increase customer satisfaction.

If the customer is to be given the power to judge, evaluate, and alter the nature of the services provided, then the fundamental grounds of a quasi-profession — the right to control the moral terms of the work, the nature of mistakes and the characteristic etiquette surrounding the interaction — are undercut. Occupations, once given a mandate, believe it is within their authority to define the nature of work and to hold out judgments of competence (Hughes 1971). A customer or consumer orientation is appropriate if the consumer has the skill, knowledge, and willingness to risk consequences of a slightly risky decision but inappropriate when the consumer cannot judge and is held at law to be unable to judge or when his or her self-interest supersedes the public interest. If customer satisfaction is weighed heavily, then market forces may substitute for values, judgment, discretion, and forbearance of others' flaws and weaknesses, the very mobilizing touchstones that make policing and other civil justice roles humane and tolerable in a mass democratic society.

TQM seeks to increase managerial flexibility. Implementation of a TQM scheme, as with all reforms, hinges upon essentially managerial decisions. It will be carried out via top-down commands and orders, often associated with implicit or explicit punishment and persuasion. What goals of policing are being mutually discussed and implemented? What is the role of the worker in setting formal written goals and objectives?

It appears that if TQM were to be adopted, through the use of focus groups, "quality circles," and shared generation of performance indicators and objectives, the responsibility for external evaluation would remain with command. It would be yet another attempt by top command to control the patrol officer, to co-opt officers to a pseudo-democratic approach while encouraging self-surveillance, internalized controls, reduced control over the conditions of work (unions and reduction of procedural guarantees for certain offenses), and a false sense of public accountability.

Police produce many things for many people and are differentially accountable to them. "Citizens" is a label, not an acting unit; they do not exist as a social group and wield no power or legitimate authority. Police are not accountable to citizens.

TQM values nonmonetary rewards such as pride, quality, dignity, and teamwork. The idea that workers can be converted to value symbolic rewards over monetary rewards assume that they adopt the cultural values of management and that these are shared. There is no evidence that a large number of police chiefs are willing to share command or have done it. Experiments with TQM, such as those in Madison, Wisconsin, have been top-down innovations, ordered from outside, or carried out in service-oriented departments. The very fact that the few large departments that have introduced TQM have encountered strong employee resistance suggests that it has elements of managerial arrogation; of power, not shared responsibility and accountability with officers. Major efforts at TQM, involving goal setting, quality circles, and teamwork in the London Metropolitan Police under Sir

Kenneth Newman and, under Chief Couper in Madison, were summarily abandoned when they left office.

Proponents claim that reduced operating costs might result from TQM, in part because fewer errors would be found after the fact, yet it is unclear how TQM in and of itself might reduce costs. The police, except with respect to selling off seizures or creating large escrow accounts and traffic tickets, have little potential to generate profits. A police budget is relatively fixed, permits little shifting of money across categories, and involves secret discretionary funds that are off the budget and used by top command to fund special investigations, internal affairs matters and narcotics buys.[19] Individual officers can do little to reduce costs. Cost control is by definition a top management, not a worker, function. Unit activities, arrests, traffic tickets, seizures, and clearances are given no precise monetary value or cost, so outputs cannot be accurately compared across units or departments. The relatively fixed costs of policing (buildings, vehicles, salaries, retirement, and benefits), like those of corrections, are vast and almost irreducible. Cost savings can be effectuated only by further rationing of services (Lipsky 1980). Externalities, such as the standing operating costs of defending and settling civil suits, are not controlled by the police but determined by city officials, attorneys, and negotiators. Savings in these categories have no direct bearing on police operating costs, although violent, reckless policing can radically increase the costs of a city through an increase in suits, a rise in insurance costs, and attorney's fees.

In summary, the quasi-economic concepts advocated for police reform are misleading. Slang and buzz words, like the misplaced metaphors of war and sport applied to policing, are dehumanizing. The "business of the police" is not "business". TQM hides managerial aims and may not advance demo-cratic policing. It may serve to undermine unions' ability to argue for legalistic protections, civil procedures, and tolerance. It will serve to rationalize firing and downsizing on the grounds of efficiency, good business, or productivity.

While the community policing movement could reform authority and create opportunities for officers to redefine their roles, TQM as presently applied may not delegate further power to officers or citizens but defend the present authority of the top command. Community policing echoes some of the pleas of reform implicit in TQM.

Parallel Themes in Police Reform

Though the community policing reform movement within policing is a powerful source of innovation and change, it has borrowed a management philosophy that intends to rationalize downsizing, flattening the organizational hierarchy, reducing paperwork, and decentralizing decision making (Maguire 1997). This is consistent with the TQM approach.

Recall first that researchers for the past twenty years have urged increased efficiency and effectiveness in policing (Wolfe and Heaphy 1975; Clarke and Hough 1980, Forst et al. 1976), absent any agreement on what either concept might measure or imply in policing practice. The currently fashionable language of economics and management used by command personnel to describe police functions, command obligations, and planning conjures a metaphoric imagery: policing as a hard-driving, profit-making business, a lean machine, that competes for market share and profits while carefully monitoring and modifying its strategies and tactics to enhance its advantages. The following uproven claims have been made about community policing:

1. Innovations, such a computer-assisted dispatch, are advocated on the grounds that they will increase efficiency or reduce costs (Hough 1980a 1980b; Tien and Colton 1979), and will even reduce calls when used in concert with community policing.
2. Community policing programs are claimed to be a cost-effective means of delivering service to customers while remaining sensitive to community needs.
3. Community policing's advocates argue that it enhances crime fighting, while reestablishing the territorial or neighborhood basis for police accountability (Moore and Trojanowicz 1988).
4. Coproduction of order it is claimed, is something like a marketing conspiracy between buyers and sellers.
5. The demand for policing is inelastic, and there is a limited market in security within which "firms" compete to sell or market their "services" to a limited number of groups who can, will, or might pay. This means that the functions carried out within such a market are somehow mutually exclusive, or "substitutable," rather than complementary and additive.
6. Community policing will reduce centralized hierarchy and expand the decision-making authority of local commanders (Maguire 1997)

These six comprise a mantra of pseudoeconomics, but no evidence exists for any of the claimed benefits.

Variations in call volume have never been demonstrated to be connected to community policing because they are produced disproportionately by areas of the city that are highly disorganized, lack phones, and are dependent on police for many services such as emergency medical assistance and conflict mediation. Since call volume is reduced by 50 percent within departments, and perhaps another 25 percent of jobs assigned are never cleared in big cities, call volume is not a function of demand but of a reduction in transaction costs (P. K. Manning 1988).

The related claim that CAD reduces paperwork is unproven. Paperwork, more detailed and rationally organized records Management Information Systems and its correlates, are in constant tension in the traditional modes of policing which emphasize closing incidents with minimal written records. These tensions between "The work" and "paper reality" have increased since the introduction of computer-assisted dispatching in the early 1970s. Computers, mobile digital terminals, and computerized record-keeping systems can reduce paperwork by using direct data entry and have led to claims that paperless policing will soon emerge through the use of mobile digital terminals, laptops in vehicles, and a fully computerized law enforcement computer network.

The most successful and closely evaluated community policing reform is Chicago's CAPS (Chicago Alternative Policing Strategy) (Skogan and Harnett 1997). According to Skogan and Harnett, police accounted for 25 percent of the city budget in 1991. The budget increased by 57 million dollars in 1992 (a rise of 9.7 percent, to a total of 686 million). The 1994 budget included funding for an additional 470 officers (above normal attrition) and 25 million to be raised by bond sales. In 1993, the program was launched with these new costs and staffing patterns that now included MBAs in each district and a mayoral office to ensure responsiveness from city agencies. The most innovative and successful feature of this program is reinventing urban machine politics by using the police as a conduit for city services such as street repair, sign and light replacement, noise control, and animal control (p. 56). Because citizens are linked to governance through the police, the exchanges that create obligation, sustain commitments, and symbolize concern are recoated daily by service-provision. The fear of corruption that drove earlier reformers has been replaced by a fear of loss of authority and taxpayers' support for municipal costs.

Unfortunately, there is little evidence of coproduction of order, increased accountability, or direct citizen establishment of priorities, objectives, or programs (Rosenbaum 1986; Skogan 1988; Skogan and Harnett 1967 ch. 7).

Policing is not guided by rational allocation of personnel by city management or by top command. Hirings and firings reflect general changes in the economy, the tax base, and other matters out of management control. Officers are assigned to posts on the basis of some combination of career aims, needs, personal politics, and programmatic support from external sources (HUD, Community Oriented Police Services, Department of Justice, COPS, or other federal grants). Fluctuations in personnel levels are, perhaps unfortunately, unrelated to changing social problems, city composition, or training or personnel needs. Community policing programs are in fact labor-intensive, and decentralized decision making may require more staff, supervision, and infrastructure. Chicago employs a cadre of civilians and an MBA in each of its twenty-five districts to coordinate budgets and planning.

Policing worldwide has a narrow range of levels and is the "flattest" modern hierarchy (Bayley 1994, 62). In Australia, two middle ranks have been eliminated, and the rank of chief superintendent was discarded in the United Kingdom The captain rank was eliminated in Chicago. The problem of policing is not hierarchy — the number of levels between the top command and the street; it is coordinating officers with unreviewed decision-making power that is rooted in tradition and the common law.

Community policing aims to increase the flexibility of officers to define, act upon, and solve problems, urges them to initiate problem-solving exercises, yet provides them with little or no training, supervision, or evaluation in such work and adds to discretion without accountability to supervising sergeants, citizens, or the polity. The accountability claim is totally unsubstantiated.

Emphasis on decentralized decision making is combined with the concurrent rationalization of police budgeting by city managers and pressures from National Institute of Justice and academic researchers to introduce rational tools (computer mapping, crime analysis units, budgeting, and management by objectives). Decentralization is inconsistent with the rhetoric of efficiency since it increases transaction costs. It has no consistent effects on policing and may lead to fragmentation of command and control.

On the other hand, the demand for police accountability creates pressures for more detailed, publicly available records of decisions and the bases for these decisions. This in turn shapes record keeping and supervision and can lead to concealing and protecting organizational secrets (Shils 1956). The "publicity effect" — the consequence of pressures for public accountability and of the Freedom of Information Act — has been felt in the private sector. Public interest in civilian review boards, complaint systems, and independent police commissions seems to be growing, and these require written contemporaneous records, not copies of easily manipulated, shaped, rewritten, recopied, erased, or otherwise modified computer files.

Specialization, a final source of concern for community policing and TQM, is rather limited in policing, since from 75 to 90 percent of most forces are in patrol (although specialization increases with scale) (Bayley 1994, 61). Detective work brings with it prestige, a salary and rank increase, and considerable freedom and nonuniform dress. Detectives have successfully avoided being integrated into community policing schemes, and in virtually every evaluated program (Rosenbaum 1994; Skogan and Harnett 1997) they stand outside the evaluation.

Ironically, investigative work is perhaps best suited to some form of outsourcing, contract work, or team efforts between patrol and investigators, because it is work based on processed and formatted, secondary and tertiary information (Manning and Hawkins 1987). The imposition of crime analysis units and other formal links between patrol and detective work increases the potential for measurement of outputs as a ratio to resources. How well this serves the other pressures from communities — victim support, better feedback on case developments and consultation with victims and witnesses, as well as the socioemotional work done by detectives when interviewing victims and witnesses — is yet unanswered.

Summary

Let us briefly summarize the principal sociological objections to applying the language and concepts of modern business to policing Policing is seen as a service, a distributional activity that reallocates collective goods. Yet police services are not fully elastic, and citizen demand, although elastic, is not permitted to expand beyond the limits set privately and backstage by police. The police continue to pattern the rationing of service as before and to dramatize the ostensible efficacy of their actions. The police do not serve lawbreakers or those who cause disorder; they constrain them regardless of their market preferences and choices. They arrest people, keep a jail, and send people to court regardless of their status as customers of the service side of policing — the side that includes paperwork, insurance forms, burglary and stolen car reports, assistance in emergencies, traffic regulation and parking, and what might be called "miscellaneous dirty work" such as chasing wild or escaped animals, disposing of bodies, delivering death notices to families, cleaning up streets of glass and metal after road accidents, and modulating disputes.

Ironically, as long as police exercise authority and violence in the name of the state they will be feared and loathed (appropriately) by some segments of any community. They represent this violence potential to all, but their actions are differentially targeted. They act proactively primarily against the lower classes — the marginal and the criminal. Police exercise violence and will be periodically unpopular, the target of protest, and viewed ambivalently. Thus, the econimic/market metaphor, which emphasizes choice and demand, is inadequate to understanding those services that are not chosen by an individual but serve the interests of the state as the police define them. These include the power to regulate, to arrest, to fine, to incarcerate, and to use deadly force. The economic conception emphasizes the service, choice, and demand management aspects of policing but denies the central fact of policing: its use of violence in the interests of the state (Bittner 1990). Members of the public are not individually served; they are not customers because they do not exercise a choice in how policing is mobilized against them; they are not clients, because they do not pay directly for individual services (with some exceptions); and they cannot judge easily the quality and quantity of service that should be allocated. Thus, the use of business rhetoric by reformers is misleading, irresponsible and even destructive of the traditional service role of the police, especially in urban areas that are police-dependent.

In the context of the present struggle for police reform several images are competing for salience. TQM, as an example of economistic reforms, substitutes new versions of managerial control for previous rule-bound bureaucratic approaches. Evidence suggests that businesses are less fettered by laws, rules, and procedures than are public agencies (Jackall 1988). The net result of the adoption of business procedures would appear to be substitution of an inappropriate economic metaphor for changing and evaluating traditional police practices. This is a veneer on traditional practices and the violence mandate that remains.

❑ THE PUBLIC-PRIVATE DIALECTIC

We have seen that public and private policing share many features and functions, and that many of the differences in costs, management, efficiency, and effectiveness have been assumed and not demonstrated empirically. The vague claim that private security excels in investigative work, risk reduction, loss protection, and crime prevention, is not substantiated by strong and consistent research. The claim that public policing, once in place, replaces self-help on the one hand and organized citizens' groups on the other holds little purchase on the facts. The crime-control penal-strategy claims by public police reveal mixed findings. Looking at privatization of discrete functions — at what is done by whom and at what costs — is perhaps more revealing than characterizing entire organizations.

Developments in public and private policing suggest a dialectic between self-help, private policing and governmental social control that has existed since establishment of the public police in the early nineteenth century. Even the dominant pattern, increasing formal state control, is not linear, coherent, unified, and consistent across all institutions (Cohen 1985, ch. 2). Development does not inevitably result in the accretion of power, resources, personnel, and legitimacy to governmental social control, or to the "hollowing out of the state" (Cohen 1985; Johnston 1992, 214–15). We are in an era of expansion of some modes of control and contraction of others, and the resulting tensions are seen in both public and private policing and their mixed function status.

Tensions in Policing

Previous historical studies of policing, with a few exceptions, such as Johnston's (1992), tend to adopt an ideological position which sees the development of policing from the perspective of public policing (see Rock 1983; Shearing 1992). Modern urban public policing is a tacit model or paradigm against which the degree of privatization is measured and constitutes a background for private policing (Pririe 1988; Steel and Heald 1984; Saunders and Harris 1990). This patterning is perhaps understandable, given the symbolic hegemony of the public police in the collective consciousness, their association with legal norms, state legitimacy and prestige, and the myths of crime control they have developed and nurtured and that they sustain. The public police mandate (P. K. Manning 1997, ch. 4) is a major constraint upon the growth of formalized private policing and the expansion of other forms of self-help. In other words, pure types of policing do not exist empirically, and all forms of policing are in some form of interaction in the context of modern, transnational, or global capitalism. The little theaters of policing, emerging in development, take part in the larger theater of emergent social organization.

The Interconnection of Police Functions

Policing is a legitimate, formal mode of social control utilizing the penal style. The several forms of policing utilize a mix of styles of control (Black, 1980), strategies (Reiss 1983, 1984), and tactics. In action, policing acts as third-party regulation or governance of social relations: a means to inspect, evaluate, and respond to behavior on the basis of norms using a range of styles of control with the force of authority. This authority may entail, as it does for all citizens under specified conditions, the right to use fatal force. These generalizations apply to all forms of policing.

Let us review the six elements of policing discussed earlier. The first element is the source of authority to act or react and relevant justifications for this authority; the second is the formal basis for obligation to act and by extension the locus of accountability; the third is the domain of stated operational interest or the field in which action is anticipated — it is premonitory and anticipatory as well as reactive; the fourth element is the source and kind of payments and/or rewards given controllers (this may be linked to the mode of budgeting employed); the fifth encompasses the length, content, and focus of the training provided, the character of recruit screening, and the recruitment pattern; and the sixth is the functional role of the controller(s).

These six elements, like a rope of associated ideas, can be variously assembled. Simple binary distinctions, such as those between public and private policing, or between policing and self-help, are highly misleading. Although Table 2.1 suggested a tidy divide, this division does not exist empirically.

The source of authority within private policing, especially in semipublic space and after apprehension, is always negotiated. Public police come into factories and arrest with permission, and private police investigate, surveil, and control people outside work and in public spaces. They enter homes, search them, and seize property. The law in most serious cases is invoked by private police in cooperation with public forces.

The obligation to act to intervene in all forms of policing is problematic, intuitive, and situational, as Bittner has argued, but private policing emphasizes prevention and anticipation of crimes, or modification of the circumstances in which they arise so that they will be less likely or reduced in their consequences. This requires investigation, systematic intelligence, and informants and sometimes entails undercover work or hired agents. Contracts and subcontracts for such work may be given to other agencies, thus expanding the agency problem while reducing in-house costs. In the emphasis upon problem solving and prevention, private policing parallels public policing in the dilemmas it faces when it undertakes proactive enforcement.

The locus of accountability in all forms of policing is blurred as old common-law defenses against liability and prosecution in America are fading fast, and insurance, accreditation, and the civil law of torts (wrongful acts) reduce the threshold of individual and organizational responsibility. Public police being investigated for untoward conduct are now often subject to three or four kinds of examination: departmental investigation via internal affairs (and perhaps an independent investigation by other command officers including the chief in some cases); official departmental quasi-judicial hearings and sanctions; civil suits and criminal investigations based or both state and federal law. Some prosecutors (based on allegations of civil rights violations, for example). Perhaps the most obvious difference is that employment rights and job security tend to be less well established in private employment, and turnover, unlike that in police departments, is very high at the lower levels. Unionized policing, common outside the south, further protects officers' job security. The interests and stated interests that are at risk and protected vary, even in large corporations with international business.

Forms of payment are relatively complex matters if one takes into account informal rewards and perks—bribery, corruption, gifts, and other forms of payment police receive routinely in some large urban departments. In addition, public police, both in and out of uniform, are employed as contract laborers and work for private groups routinely in many cities (Reiss 1988). The official source of pay may be a public agency, but gifts, fees, contracts, and grants from private groups may be processed as pay to public servants. Community policing results in a flood of gifts to individual officers, such as bulletproof vests, to units (e.g., bicycles given to bike patrol officers), or to the department for specific functions (e.g., the police athletic league) from individuals and organizations. As will be discussed below, rational budgeting, contracting, purchasing, and auditing practices remain very underdeveloped in policing. This is in part a reflection of the traditional, almost sacred, nature of the work and its general mission to protect and promote the general welfare. It is not even known how much it costs to employ, train, pay, and equip an officer in North America, to operate a patrol vehicle, or to investigate a crime (Bayley 1992b). Estimates vary. Training — length, content, and type — varies, according to most reliable information.

The sixth and final blurred distinction concerns the factors shaping the controller's role. The law increasingly casts its penumbra on officers' actions, and interventions are now rationalized by written decisions, rules, and guidelines. The formalization of policy, written and explicit, is proceeding apace, especially in key areas of police conduct such as engaging in high-speed pursuits, using fatal force, controlling violent episodes in the workplace, selecting intelligence targets, employing surveillance tactics, and using informants and undercover agents.

Variations in Modes of Policing

Variations on each of the six elements are found in both public and private police agencies. Policing is characterized by a dialectic with a dynamic, oscillating flow, and naturalistic studies are much needed to simply plot the territory. Johnston (1992) notes that distinctions between public and private policing are descriptive rather than theoretically derived. Building on, the typology of Saunders and Harris (1990), he argues that

> any assessment of privatization has to be conditional. One cannot make a blanket statement about the costs and benefits of a privatization policy without first examining the form of privatization under consideration, and the context in which it is implemented. Conventional assessment of privatization rarely takes this form, however. Proponents of the policy assume that it maximizes effectiveness, efficiency and freedom regardless of the political and organizational context. Opponents, by contrast, assume that the profit motive invariably leads to higher priced, poorer quality services. In fact, the truth is likely to be more complex and more variable than either side allows for. (P, 51)

The assumptions used to establish the types are notional, philosophical, and political and are an unlikely basis for empirical research examining the complex and variable consequences of the process of privatization. This statement implies that the base is the public police and that privatization reduces the functions of the public police. It contains no mention of the dynamics of self-help. The assumption of a public police monopoly in regard to order and force is dubious.[21] The purpose of this section is to review functions across the three types to show that *policing functions* are variously performed in this society and cohere in clusters of the elements.

Police Functions in General

Organizational Policing Consider first *organizational forms,* which are based on source of pay, client, or audience and include the classic agency problem in economics: how to maintain control over agents acting indirectly on one's behalf (Heimer 1985a, 1985b; Shapiro 1987). With regard to organized groups, policing can refer of course, to personalized activity in defense of the interests of those groups. It can also connote public policing, in which full-time uniformed officers serve and are paid by the state and work for no one else. In the context of private policing, the variations proliferate and overlap with those of public policing. Private policing can refer concretely to (1) private for-profit policing paid for directly by corporate sources, as in the case of the security division of Ford, Florida Power and Light, 3M, or the Whirlpool Corporation. It can also encompass (2) private for-profit policing, provided to corporation under contract with an agency such as Wackenhut, Pinkerton, Burns, or an alarm company and paid for by those corporations. Private policing also includes policing (3) paid for partially by a mall or organized, incorporated citizens' group and by a public entity; (4) paid for exclusively by a neighborhood association, gated community, or patrolled and/or alarmed subdivision; (5) provided by citizens using cellular phones, walkie-talkies, and CB radios and patrolling in their own cars; and (6) provided by a sheriff's department (or the RCMP in Canada) by contract to a township.

Individual Policies If one turns to policing done by *individuals* (volunteers, contracted or paid) rather than by organizations, the range of activities is considerably broader. Another pattern appears. (1) Public police are engaged in activities in the public police role for which they are paid by private sources; for example, they may be hired by private citizens, groups of citizens, or corporate groups such as the sponsors of rock concerts, sporting events, parades, and demonstrations. Many of these activities, such as providing security at an annual event, are governed by long-term contracts. Some cities, such as Boston, require construction companies to employ a uniformed police office to attend all construction sites. In contrast, Detroit requires officers to attend and supervise city festivals and parades but does not pay extra-duty pay unless the officer would otherwise be off duty. (2) Public police are hired as individuals to police, usually out of uniform, hotels, motels, gambling casinos, convention centers, and malls. In this case, the police department screens and approves the individual's request to moonlight. Some cities, such as Atlanta, must approve the work and will not permit work in establishments where liquor is served, or in some entertainment places. Others, such as Detroit announced in 1997 that they planned to permit officers in uniform to police be employed by gambling casinos. (Reiss [1995] estimates that some 25 percent of departments permit second jobs for pay.) (3) Officers in some cities (Chicago, for example) are allowed to take a second job with another police department. (4) Police reserves, cadets, and other nonsworn officers perform police duties for pay (received from the police department). (5) Some police departments (for example, San Diego) use large numbers of unpaid citizen volunteers to function in a variety of police roles. The Lansing, Michigan, department has organized senior citizens to check on truants, and the Ingham County (Michigan) sheriff has lent marked patrol vehicles to be driven by senior citizens who patrol and cite cars without disabled tags that are parked in designated disabled parking places.

Services   Increasingly, as Johnston (1992) and Bayley and Shearing (1996) have argued, police are charging directly for services such as answering alarm calls (in some cases, only false alarms are charged), policing parades, and responding to traffic accidents where fault is established. (In San Diego, the courts can order compensation for ambulance, fire, and police service at an accident.) Some police functions, such as environmental policing, are contracted for by other city agencies. In East Lansing, Michigan, an environmental and parking officer patrols the streets giving tickets for overnight parking (prohibited from 2 to 6 A.M. to facilitate winter snow ploughing) and for abandoned couches and furniture, litter, cars in yards, and noise. The police departments of San Diego and many other cities can issue environmental citations. In Lansing, Michigan, the police permit a private agency to pursue bad check writers and keep the money collected. Businesses advertise that they subscribe to the "Better Check Cashing Corporation" and warn customers against writing bad checks. The police in turn do not investigate these crimes. Increasingly, civilians are employed by the police. Approximately 27 percent of police employees are civilians (Bayley 1994, 90). This percentage varies widely by departments and tends to be correlated with size. This growth is primarily in computer services, record keeping, and research and development.

Police and private security organizations engage in joint transactions, ranging from ad hoc individual operations to long-term, semiformal cooperative agreements (Draper 1979, ch. 6; South 1989, 87–95; Geller and Morris 1992; Ericson and Haggerty 1997, 172–176ff). This is in part facilitated by the circulation of retired police officers into security firms. These may include former CIA agents in risk assessment divisions of large corporations like 3M or in corporations that evaluate risks for companies planning foreign investments, joint ventures, or construction. Credit investigations may be undertaken by companies like TRW and can involve informal cooperation between public and private agencies or between corporations and private investigators. FBI and Secret Service agents hold many executive positions in corporate security. State and local police often form their own security or alarm businesses or join local security firms after retirement. Police mount joint operations to patrol parking lots during the holiday shopping season make or longer-term arrangements to provide side-by-side mini stations with offices of the public police and mall security, as in the Lloyd Center in Portland, Oregon.

The space is donated by the owners of the shopping center. The FBI charges local police agencies for services such as fingerprint identification and sells forensic services to local and state agencies. In the United Kingdom, two specialized forms of privatization are present — hiring guards and personnel for criminal justice services and granting them special powers as constables for this purpose (Johnston 1992, 108–13). Public bodies, such as the armed services and federal agencies, hire private security guards to protect installations and bases around the world. The U.S. federal government is the largest single employer of private security personnel (some thirty-six thousand of the 1 million private security officers in the United States).

In part because of budget reductions, shrinkage due to attrition and retirement, and shrinking-center city populations, the police are considering sloughing some of their functions. In the most dramatic form this has meant refusing to dispatch an officer to some types of calls for service taking reports of missing persons or missing or stolen cars by phone taking an insurance report by phone or delaying attending to noise and other nuisance calls and prioritizing types of calls. Although formal modes of setting priorities are built into CAD systems, in practice everything is sent down and officers on the ground set all meaningful priorities (P. K. Manning 1988). Many reports from citizens can be submitted by fax or mail or phoned in. Detroit has used a special "garbage" car to attend to low-priority nuisance calls. Less dramatic have been the use of faxes to send and receive accident reports, permitting reports to be taken over the phone rather than in person (e.g., for cold burglaries), encouraging citizens to use voice mail to contact officers, and assigning special community officers to a given area (Landing, Michigan). Police contract out for some services, such as training, computer installation and maintenance, and auto repair.

Privatizing of selected functions within the public justice system proceeds apace. Some are listed by Johnston (1992, 108–13). These include contracting out management of parolees on electronic tethers (the monitoring and surveillance equipment is operated by a private corporation) immigration control (in the United Kingdom) handling bail and remand and transporting prisoners between jail, prisons, and court.[22]

Activities and Functions of Private Police

We can consider this kaleidoscope by giving it another turn and asking, are the activities private security once did now done by them?

1. *Guarding and protecting private property and space.* These types of functions range from retail and public security in schools and hospitals to

controlling access to plants, parking lots, and secure areas within organizations. The private police have traditionally focused on guarding and protecting property via motorized or foot patrol or fixed points. This is now accomplished by individuals who watch parking lots, buildings, and warehouses from a distance using television monitors and sophisticated sound-detecting alarm systems. Bar codes, passcards, and computerized systems of access control and monitoring substitute for guards and locked doors in many large corporations (e.g., Ford Motor Company in Dearborn, Michigan). This access-control function has been increasingly outsourced to Pinkerton or other large companies. In 1997, GM decided to outsource its guard function to Wackenhut, an example of load shedding from one corporation to another within the private sphere. The security function is shared, as mentioned above, in many malls and shopping areas.

2. *Guarding intellectual property.* The security division within a corporation or an "outsourced" corporation hired to protect company assets is typically charged with protecting the corporate good name. Increasingly, it appears, corporate good will, a good name, and symbolic property such as formulas, plans, long-term strategies, computer programs, and information are defined as property. They represent a domain of struggle and conflict over rights, intelligence and espionage contests, and internal turf battles with corporations. Legal departments and department of human resources, security, accounting, and computing all have interests in these symbolic properties. These symbolic assets entail new kinds of risks and risk-management strategies, because they may be stolen or copied by competitors, national and international, as well as by agents of foreign countries. This engages the federal government in the struggle to protect intellectual property — software that has multiple (defense and commercial) potential — and in the information war. Information may be taken without a trace, for example, by computer experts hired by another company. This area of security has been dominated by computer experts, risk managers, and human resource divisions, or even media relations, rather than by the security division per se. Industrial espionage, surveillance, and intelligence functions have emerged in distinctive units within corporations, sometimes distinct from security on the organizational table. As economic competition substitutes for cold war anticommunism, and a information war is being waged by the Defense Department, the CIA, and the FBI, intelligence functions will shift to economic espionage, and more attention will be given to information control (Sarbin 1997). Conversely, the trade and exchange of information and the game of blocking information, seeking it, and using it for security purposes serves to further commodify

information. Organizations such as TRW gather, systematize, and sell credit information.

3. *Participating in risk-management activities.* Risk management, pioneered by insurance companies, has shifted the focus of all forms of policing away from punishment for crime, losses, or offenses to the management of known losses. It is increasingly difficult for the security division to estimate costs of reduced or prevented loss accurately enough to justify budgetary expenditures, and accounting, computer services, and human resources divisions are undertaking the assessments. Many new forms of crime are deeply embedded in computerized accounting and budgeting systems, and old crimes, such a pilfering and employee loss and shrinkage, are monitored with bar coding systems, video cameras, and television screens.

4. *Information analysis and processing.* Intelligence functions — that is, the systematic gathering, processing, and analyzing of information in order to anticipate a loss, risk, or act of terrorism — are rising in significance.

5. *Surveillance via electronic means.* As electronic surveillance, audio and visual, becomes more compact, cheaper, and more mobile, it is used both to prevent employees and agents of other companies from stealing information or property and to gather intelligence on other companies. This capacity to gather intelligence stimulates counterespionage, deception, misrepresentation, and lies on behalf of employers (Draper 1979, ch. 4). This area of public-private cooperation — for example sharing files, equipment, or investigators — circumvents civil liberties and due process protections that surround criminal investigations but not privately funded investigations (South 1989, 98–99). Advanced databases that can be accessed or shared raise substantial worries about networks of surveillance and probing into private relations (Lyon 1994; Marx 1988).

6. *Investigations of crimes committed on private space or by employees.* Private police have also long investigated incidents that would be labeled crime if they were committed outside corporate boundaries (the blandly named "investigative function"). These include such crimes as arson, terrorism, assault, harassment, and theft that the acts take place on company property or are committed by employees and can range from computer crime, fraud, embezzlement, and other UCR crimes, if UCR labels are used, to terrorism, spreading computer viruses, and misuse of company assets. Investigations of such crimes, either after the fact or in anticipation of them might be labelled and undertaken variously — through interviewing and investigation, undercover work, paid informants, forming liaisons with the public police, and hiring detectives from agencies or known and trustworthy individuals like ex-FBI agents. With reductions in personnel and downsizing

generally, less experienced and educated employees now staff security firms. Investigative work is often contracted for.

7. *Crime prevention, risk management, and loss reduction.* These functions provide the ostensible rationale for employing private security in corporations. The tasks can range from working on employee theft and reducing shrinkage to handling more complex questions such as designing the security system of new premises, installing alarm systems, and providing physical security of goods. Thus, companies that service alarms and surveillance equipment consult on security matters. Conversely, with the adoption of problem-solving, situational crime prevention (Clarke 1980) and efforts at prevention like DARE, public police consider crime prevention a new tool, and it is very popular. These activities shade over into community cleanups and other civic activities in which the police now participate.

8. *Applied violence.* Physical violence, now that strikes and union agitation have all but disappeared, is less needed. The control and patrol of set spaces have been the core of corporate private security, and the protection of executives remains important.

9. *Transporting and securing cash and property.* This is one of the traditional functions around which private policing arose, and it remains a core function of security companies such as Well Fargo, Pinkerton, and local security companies. Armed courier services, transporting money, servicing banks (and now, ATMs), and providing alarm services and property security complement the investigative services.[23]

10. *Feudal loyalty and fealty.* Corporate security has historically been tied to backstage work that combines bodyguarding, the occasional application of protective violence, and doing miscellaneous odd jobs for corporate officers and top management. Policing in general includes such functions, and they are an essential part of the politics of police organizations.[24] The chief's office in any large city department includes drivers, bodyguards for the chief and mayor or other dignitaries, and ambitious future command officers, among others.

❏ DILEMMAS AND CONTRADICTIONS

A series of dilemmas arises when traditional policing functions are designed to make a profit, whether these are internal management or external (strategies and tactics of policing) functions. The source of pay and other dimensions differentiating public from private policing are important, but the driving force of profit alters the fundamental outlines of policing. How and why this alteration occurs and its extent remain empirical ques-

tions. The following discussion identifies police functions that are anticipated to change and describes how introducing rationalized fiduciary
structures (with associated managerial skill, budgeting, and evaluation consistent with other for-profit corporations) might change policing.

Dilemmas

Table 2.1 outlined the elements and dimensions for comparison
between public and private police. These give rise to dilemmas as functions
are transferred, discarded, shifted about, and reorganized. These are dilemmas of the transformation of policing since they describe dilemmas of
policing in general.

Seven questions about policing organize this section.

1. What are the nature and locus of accountability?
2. What performance indicators and measurements exist?
3. How can one determine efficiency and effectiveness?
4. What are the expected changes in the quality of police service?
5. What are the risks and values of decreased social distance between
   police and the public?
6. How will citizens' needs versus their capacity to pay and resultant
   stratification effects alter the distribution of services and their
   source(s)?
7. What are the known risks and benefits of the commodification of
   security?

Accountability

The long debate about the kind and locus of accountability for the
police has continued for almost two hundred years. Debate centers on the
questions of whether the controls should be internal — in the form of an
audit, a internal affairs unit, or better training — or external, such as civilian
review or complaints boards, general mechanisms of governmental review
such as city council, mayor, or city manager supervision, a police commission or human relations committee in city government, or a consultative
committee at the local and citywide level. Local, county, and state laws are
now joined by a wider range of civil remedies and federal laws that apply
to states in areas of discrimination, civil rights, and procedural guarantees.
Little research on these mechanisms exists, and variations in local practices
and traditions are great. It is perhaps fair to generalized and state that

though the law offers little prospective guidance, civil suits have increasingly become ex post facto means to control police behavior (Del Carmen 1991).

Private policing is constrained by internal corporate structures and practices, by civil and administrative law, and by company policies on, for example, matters of gathering industrial intelligence, use of undercover agents, and secret surveillance of employees. The question of loyalty remains salient, since loyalty to top management is critical to the private functions security performs, but this is made more complicated when the security services are provided by contract. Being regulated on the job is probably consented to as a result of employment. If private security is offered, a choice exists: exit (leaving), voice (protesting and seeking change) or loyalty (staying with the program) (Hirschman 1970).

Market choices would govern the consumer's shifts in security systems used if privatization were to increase. Market dynamics of choice, costs, satisfaction, and consumer demand would rule the growth or decline of given services and given agencies. Territorial and regional differences, as in all local government, would arise. How huge corporations are to be held accountable for their services, other than through contracts, is yet unanswered (Shearing 1992, 421–26).

Performance Indicators and Measurements

The general problems of efficiency and effectiveness were discussed in the previous section. The problems with performance indicators are unresolved tensions between (1) performance measurement(s) rooted in organizational practices governed by tacit conventions (e.g., burglary arrests, traffic tickets), (2) subjective measures of quality of life (satisfaction with service, numbr of complaints), dependent upon customer satisfaction and consumption of services, and (3). matters of coproduction or partnerships that vary by neighborhood, division, subdivision, city area, and region.

The measurement of performance — selecting the performances to be monitored and evaluated and applying standards such as efficiency (best use of resources) and effectiveness (accomplishing stated ends) — presumes that a consensus on measurement procedures and concepts exits, along with a capacity to employ those procedures within organizations and an ability to produce feedback and corrections based on these systems of monitoring. Furthermore, it assumes that they have transcendent validity. Only in narrowly defined areas, where policy, measurement, and feedback have been articulated in American policing, have policy-driven results been demonstrated (P. K. Manning 1997). In short, there is no evidence that the capacity to be monitored and measured is now in place in public or private policing. COPS grants, with built-in evaluation procedures, will encourage the police to build this infrastructure.

Efficiency and Effectiveness

These concepts and their slippery quality, or context-based meaning, are discussed above. The problems that arise from context in policing concern the relative values of freedom, procedural protections, potential for inequitable policing practices, and the impact of demand monitored and constrained only by "street-level bureaucrats" (Lipsky 1980). (Officers are at least close to the decisions made while managers.) are more distant and often "out of touch." It remains only to say that no research has established the parameters along which these could be measured in policing.

Quality of Service

Satisfaction with quality may be a misleading concept. Clearly, citizens are not consumers or customers: they rarely choose to be arrested, to be given a ticket, to be stopped and searched, or to have their houses searched. The primary product of policing is ordering, with its implicit dimension of the threat of force, and this, in turn, rests on trust. Politicians may demand service that serves unequally. The latest movement in community policing, the combination of tactical street pressure and zero tolerance, focusing on the poor, the homeless, the mentally ill, and the disorderly and powerless (Kelling and Coles 1996), is a means-oriented tactic. It illustrates the insidious ways in which control and quality can be converted into tools for repressive police action. Cities have begun to combine private policing, city agencies, criminal law, and municipal regulations to close and seize crack houses (Lansing, Michigan; San Diego, California), wall off streets to prevent traffic for prostitution (Lansing, Michigan), and evict tenants from public housing. Here, questions of justice for whom must arise.

Reduced Social Distance and Corruption

Since the mid-eighties, the question of corruption, or differential treatment of individuals by officers on the basis of informal rewards, has been discussed in connection with community policing. This arises because the presumption of objectivity and equity is explicit in public service. It is not an assumption of commodified security services. As O'Malley (1996) notes, neo-libertarianism reverses figure and ground and argues that "efficient" (not fair or equitable) government should arise from market forces; governments should, like private relations in capitalism, be governed by economic matters (Shearing 1992, n. 418). The market is the paradigm by which the operation, structure, and processes of delivery of goods and services can be evaluated. In this sense, corruption becomes a matter of illegal business practice, or simply put, a matter of how far protection to the consumer is extended in a given industry. When the notion of being served is dependent on paying, the interests of the employer are clearly at odds with the broader social good. South (1989, 99) puts this in the most stark way: "The further privatization of criminal justice system services — and the private appropriation of their symbolic affinity with the provision of *public* services by the state — must be challenged and resisted on the grounds of tradition and legitimacy, legality and accountability, and ethics and morality."

Distribution of Services

Will increased privatizing of policing functions that serve the public (rather than the major client, the government itself in the United Kingdom and United States) stretch the stratification system? That is, will services be minimized or withdrawn from some areas, groups, and large areas of cities? Will differential treatment based on ability to pay and bargain increase victimization and property losses? Will a market in security arise parallel to the market in education advocated by some neoliberals through the use of vouchers, choice of server, and private police options? The community policing movement has as stated policy implicit local standards of policing rather than egalitarian service. The actual operation of reactive policing remains democratic in the sense of equal response to calls (Shearing 1984), while clearly, as "hot spots" research shows (Sherman 1992) and known police practice demonstrates, police focus attention on lower-class, crime-ridden areas for proactive work and problem solving. Crime control has costs beyond crime control.

Risks and Benefits of Commodification

The idea that security, a social psychological concept, can be bought and sold, or more accurately that the means by which it is notionally to be ensured can be bought, is called the "commodification of security" (Spitzer and Scull 1977a, 1977b; see Tunnell 1992). The private security industry, focused on patrols, alarm devices, and other forms of electronic surveillance of property and inner spaces, has always served propertied interests, those who own property and could afford extra protection. The issue of equality arises if democratic policing, whatever the distribution of personnel and service, is eroded by shrinking budgets, attrition (through retirement, disability, layoffs, or firings), tax or spending limits, and/or withdrawal of support for public services.

These seven points highlight the transformation of policing, because a dialectic between public and private police always exists, as well as a partial overlap in functions and activities. The question is how social values and beliefs are interwoven with concerns about the quality of life, policing services, and crime control. What social costs result from increases in the market share of private police, or conversely, reductions in the resources of the public police? In general, I view them as too high relative to the gain in social integration.

The impact of economic thinking on criminal justice, public policy, and sociolegal studies and the law has been great in the last thirty years. Arguments for the efficiency of the common law have animated the law and economics scholars for twenty years; critiques of the inefficiency of policing, courts, and corrections have been current since the President's Crime Commission (1967) published its findings; and implicit in the neoliberal critique of the public sector generally is that the consumer should be responsible for coproduction of order and rational choices, and the police, in turn, should apply economic rationality to their management.

Product differentiation and differentiation of services have already evolved in private policing. The workings of profit and protection and market forces already shape some of the services. Those shaped are significant, but equally significant are services that involve trust, service, loyalty and backstage operations. Furthermore, one of the most volatile matters now facing private policing is its lack of an intelligence capacity and an ability to respond to crimes of trust violation, fraud, and industrial espionage. The costs of intelligence, as the CIA well knows, cannot be easily estimated, since intelligence involves discovering, validating, and creating the future, as well as securing symbolic property and investigating its loss. Growth in police authority is required in areas where market forces are somewhat ambiguous — the market in symbolic representations has long been the world of advertising and the mass media, not of police. Conversely, private security has grown in the past through guarding and protecting property, a function now being carried out by electronic means with a few glazed-eyed employees monitoring gray screens. Other growth areas are "containment within the C.J. system" (Johnston 1992, 108–13) — privatized corrections (Nuzum 1998), and the use of contracts and outsourcing to employ guards, drivers, and clerks (Howard League *Newsletter* May 1997).

Economic arguments for efficiency in public services are often estimates based on conventional (economic) assumptions about choice and
values, processes modeled by formulas, and using objective metrics, usually
money, as the outcome measure. The Atkinson Report exemplifies misleading aspects of such research and its essentially nonempirical nature. Subjective factors that are critical in criminal justice policies and practices, ideas
like justice, fear, satisfaction, and — the central ones — crime and costs, are
usually measured by fiat or converted into a metric that suggests facile
comparisons. If, for example, one wants to measure fear of crime operationally, then reported fear, actions to defend oneself, and changes in routines
— after controlling for age, race, and past victimization — show that fear is
the greatest among those least at risk for victimization of personal crimes
and property crimes, while those most victimized in both respects are the
least fearful. There is no consensus on the key matter of fear of crime, or
whether fear of crime is equally or more important than actual reported
crime as a police concern. The same point could be made about satisfaction
with police services — those who receive most (denied in terms of contact)
are the most negative in their evaluations.

Turning to management, it is perhaps easiest to estimate the parameters of activity, cost, and source. But consider a simple matter, crime report
processing. Assume that the police aim to broaden their services to burglary
victims, and pressures arise to write more detailed reports and to reject
fewer claims. This means that costs defined in time spent on burglary reports
will increase for dispatchers, operators, and uniformed officers, as well as
detectives. These costs in parts are simply absorbed by the "standard
operating or fixed costs of the institutions" — for example, $500,000 per car
per month. (Bayley 1992b). They might be reflected also in time budgets or
observations kept, overtime, and increases in the paperwork transmitted to
detectives and eventually to district attorneys. Costs in large part cannot be
traced. They will vanish into standard budgeting procedures and modes of
management which are highly discretionary and emphasize production, or
numbers, not the quality of the work or the service rendered. The result of
this exercise is hypothetically to increase the pass-through costs to the
police and transaction costs with the prosecuting attorneys. Perhaps more
burglars are caught, perhaps not, because the vast majority of clearances
result from "crimes taken into account" — admissions to past burglaries —
rather than from more arrested burglars. So the aim of the exercise,
broadening services to increase citizen satisfaction, may not correlate with
normal outcome measures based on costs. Any increase or decrease in
outcome measures is ambiguously defined in policing anyway, and there is

always an alternative explanation (if one is offered for crime dynamics — "Crime is up because it is summer and people are outside; crime is down because people are on vacation"). Is the current police aim to reduce known crimes (a focus on the rate), increase arrests, increase the number of criminals arrested (equivalent to reducing those at large? Pepinsky 1980) (a focus on criminals), or prevent crime? How are these matters related empirically to variations in the quality of life in an area, or to satisfaction with police services?

This example bears on the processing of routine matters, but what of the differential police attention to high politics and dramatic, high-visibility media-spectacle cases that the public, it is said, demands to have solved — the Waco-Koresh surveillance and raids, the Polly Klas kidnapping and murder case, the Megan rape and murder case (which lead to state laws requiring registration of released convicted sex offenders) case, the Jon-Benet Ramsey murder. These cases typically alter budgeting rules, divert detective attention for long periods, preoccupy management and top command, and occupy vast space in television news and newspapers. Similar attention, overtime, and strenuous police efforts accompany only two other events: the murder or attempted murder of an officer (if the suspect is other than an officer) and an escaped prisoner. All such exceptional events are viewed from the inside as central to the police mission. Though they are rare events, their management is essential to maintaining public trust. If private agencies devote their time to important cases, as defined by management or the employer, ignoring other matters, what ethics prevent disproportionate efforts on these cases, violations of privacy, and inequitable treatment of the "enemies" of employers (Draper 1979, chs. 4 and 7)?[25]

Some Anticipated Consequences

There are both individual and group consequences of applying the economic metaphor to policing. The individual level refers to implications for individuals denoted and connoted by the market language of economics applied to policing, while the group level refers to the same matters as they bear on group structure and relations.

Impacts

Consider first the *individualistic* aspects of such language. Market participation and individual choice among services are valued, and individually focused notions about how and to whom services will be rendered are consistent with deploying resources evaluated on the basis of social profit. Citizens are defined as customers or clients. Aggregated ordering of individual problems constitutes a police service area. Contracts and exchange relations are elevated at the expense of collective goods and noncontractual aspects of contracts (Macauley 1963). Shopping around for social control services and distrust of the sources of control increase. Stable and trusting relationships are established with individual service providers — the officers — rather than with the state or the organization as a whole. Money talks or is the bottom line when considering whether a practice will continue.

If the economistic metaphor is applied at the *group* level, other consequences ensue. The corporate strategy emphasizes competition, market shares, and the rise and fall of corporate profits. Strategy and tactics are used to deploy resources and are the basis for calculating the rate of return on investment. Gains in corporate profits are scrutinized on the basis of the surplus labor value that can be extracted from the human resources (people-employees). Income and earning, the bottom line, effectiveness and productivity, become watch or buzz words disconnected from precise measures of what these might mean operationally. A police product or service is produced, distributed, promoted, and sold. The value of the services rendered is calculated in economic terms; money differentiates the audiences served, the quality of the service received, and the soundness of a long-term investment strategy.

In this context, violence used against the lower classes is seen as a service to the respectable classes. The irony is perhaps that a substantial minority of policing is not chosen (it is not direct service to an individual) and is in fact coercive violence and constraint applied in the name of the state.

Advertising, the correct media, and public relations that lead to finding the right spin on any fact, take on new importance (Mawby 1997; Jackall 1988, ch. 6). Packaging and promotion, such as the billboard ads and television publicity campaigns for using 911, are intended to increase demand for police services. The result of increasing demand, given a labor-intensive industry, is that policing is privately controlled and rationed by bureaucratic means of filtering, screening, denying requests, or withholding a promised level of response (Lipsky 1980).

☐ CONCLUSIONS

Answering the question, Should the police be privatized? presupposes a perspective within which the question and answer will be posed. My part of this book draws on the dramaturgical perspective and emphasizes the drama of control, characterizes economic rhetoric and metaphor and their capacities for shaping discourse and advances definitions, types, and blurred areas of overlap in the function and meaning of policing.

My argument, in brief, embedded in the critique of economic rhetoric, is that all forms of fee for service and its many variants, the essence of the economic/free market paradigm, and extracting fees and profit from human misery or commodified needs are inconsistent with the police mandate, the nature of collective goods and their distribution, and in some sense the moral bases of collective solidarity and trust that as yet bind us.

Policing and the Political Economy

Policing requires an analysis that looks beyond policing. Recall the previous discussion about the ambiguities in the concept "police," its several components (local, state, federal, and private), and the lack of systematic criteria and databases for all policing (Cunningham and Taylor 1985). Policing is embedded in the political economy.

Political economy refers to the distribution of resources, including material goods, moral authority, and symbolic legitimacy, in line with power and authority in a society. As was argued in the first section of part 2, such matters are embedded in the landscape of subjectively derived meanings, of morality and drama, and are enacted in the little and big theatres of politics and social control. Political economy also includes the material and the symbolic, anything exchanged and differentiated within society. From the political economy arise collective memory, social boundaries, and social history. The exchange of symbols is a slippery and often misleading matter because the exchange of any commodity leaves a residue or trace that devolves to the powerful. I have argued that the police represent society, marking its sense of its self, and thus are symbolic transducers.

What is exchanged has traditionally been a moral sense — what is right, proper, moral, or even expedient. In that sense, policing always displays change: it is dynamic, expanding and contracting functions, accumulating and discarding duties. Given the inspectorial origins of policing (Bacon 1939), the evolved structure, strategy, and tactics (Reiss 1992b), based in large part on the growth of the national state and in particular the welfare state, it is not surprising that market forces shape police institutions. Their primitive origins and connections, sacred connotations, and connection to law, authority, and morality have insulated them for some time from market pressures that have altered so many public institutions from public radio to primary and secondary education. The abiding point is that the moral and sacred consistently resist rationalization and vulgarization (Fixler and Poole 1998).

The little theater of policing is predicated on a mandate of trust and legitimacy that reflects the investment of groups in the current order. Patterns of trust of the police vary by ethnicity, gender, and class, as well as by experience with policing. Ironically, of course, the mission of maintaining order is realized publicly in the attempt to control crime by focusing on places, persons, and routines. Too often policing is judged by what it is against rather than what it intends to be for.

I have argued that the crisis and turning points in policing resemble each other and that formal modes of control are in competition with informal modes, especially self-help. Historically, public police arose to provide services or control for public activities, and the argument has been made that these are unprofitable on their face since they must be sustained by taxation rather than free choice (Feeley 1970). Western democracies and the rise of the welfare state meant that inefficient services, partial attempts to redistribute symbolic benefits of the state to all, had competition only at the margins — that is, protection, especially in transportation, of large amounts of property, wealth in homes through use of alarms, and private land in general. The rise of private police parallels that rise and growth of public police (Nalla and Newman 1993, 44), with recent history suggesting that the ratio is decreasing as private security forces grow relative to public police.[27]

In many respects, Western democracies are more policed than ever, both numerically and per capita,[28] and they use a wider range of technologies that expand the capacities of smell, sight, hearing, and touch as well as thinking. Most significant in this respect are the massive increases in information technology and visual surveillance in public places. The rise and growth of policing now shadow and include alternative forms of control. The public police not only use arrest and detention — the penal style — but also mediation and referral to mediation and counseling, education and direct education through the DARE program, both formal and informal restitution, and liaisons, in the community policing mode, with housing inspectorates, public housing administrators, public health agencies, fire departments, and parks and recreation departments.

Whether the resistance to rationalization takes the form of lawsuits, social movements, riots, union activity, work stoppage and strikes by the police, or the long hours and moral fervor of police and the strong, somewhat quaint occupational culture of the patrol officer, resistence remains.

The Future

Social change and development shape societies' form or style of control. Durkheim (1964) argues, briefly stated, that societies evolve from a penal or punishment-oriented mode of control to restitution. Anthropological and cross-cultural research suggests that Durkheim refers to only the last two to three hundred years of forms of control seen in industrial democracies. Do the current movements in policing toward community policing, restitution by criminals to victims, victims' rights movements, and risk management rather than use of penal sanction indicate long-term trends? The high rates of incarceration, severe sentencing practices, less funding for social services than for corrections and police all suggest contrary trends and a fragmentation of social control (Cohen 1985). Morality and politics have independent effects on crime control expenditures and strategies that are very difficult to measure.

Does the future suggest a police focus on crime control or on prevention and secondarily on management? Sir Robert Peel, with other practical theorists of policing, Patrick Colquhoun, Henry and Joseph Fielding, and Bentham, emphasized the importance of prevention and the absence of disorder and crime, not crime control, as an indication of success.

The police cannot be expected in the near future to increase their efficacy or their visible impact on crime (as measured by victim surveys, official reports, or costs) not only because of the changing nature of crime, costs, and democratic values such as privacy, justice, and equal treatment under the law, but because the public is less concerned about crime than about security and fear. It is the pursuit of security, coupled with its designation as a product or commodity to be bought and sold, rather than crime rates per that dominates crime discourse.

What does the future hold? Some analysts argue that the issue of distinguishing public from private policing is moot, since all regulatory agencies are actual risk managers and hubs of larger communications networks. In Ericson and Haggerty's (1997) view, police are increasingly the center of information networks and are actively gathering, processing, and synthesizing information for and with other agencies — city and state government, insurance companies, fire departments, the Internal Revenue Service, credit card companies, and private security companies and manufacturers of security equipment. These transactional links make easy distinctions between types of policing quite problematic, and suggest that more precise and slightly less abstract concepts are needed.

Risk and security appear as meaningful categories when narrow notions of class and hierarchy recede in postmodern societies. Ericson and Haggerty (1997) argue that security is the abiding future focus of policing: security of territory, group identity, and the person. They link this growth to changes in social organization of mass societies toward a postmodern, individually oriented, communications-and information-based semisymbolic order. In such a society, standards are notional and fragmented, and thin networks of social control expand through networks of communication exchange rater than face-to-face exchanges. Styles of control are blurred and used by many agencies. Rationalization of policing occurs through the processing of communication in networks facilitated by computers. In this sense, Ericson and Haggerty fault those who see the police as reactive and inclined to means-oriented data. They argue that active information gathering, analyzing, and processing is already replacing the passive and reactive mode of gathering data for warehousing or storage. Observation, classification, and surveillance data are tightly linked. The police consolidate and organize information used to predict, surveil, classify, and label *in advance* groups who are crime risks, those who are *at* risk, and pursue known law-breakers.

Security is now provided as a service and both public and private groups offer it (Tunnell 1992). Rather than seeing life) as occasionally being risky, the commodification of security (Spitzer and Scull, 1977a, 1977b; Ericson and Haggerty 1997) means that like automobiles, homes, clothing, and food, security must be acquired at some cost. Security can be purchased in a market for security which sets price and costs and yields benefits. No longer is security a public or collective good to which all must contribute and from which all benefit (Samuelson 1954; Feeley 1970).

Such developments might reflect changing patterns of commitment and altruism in America in the sense that reduced willingness to pay, in part reflecting the "free-rider problem" (some persons benefit but do not pay proportionately), erodes the quality of public service and permits only those who have additional discretionary income to compete for additional security in the form of patrols, burglar alarms, security systems, and investigative services.

As security becomes a commodity to be bought and sold, marketed and contracted for, the costs and availability of services will reflect what the market will bear. Perhaps the market will expand, and the division of security labor will be renegotiated. Though many profitable functions are served now by private security augmented by data from public systems, such a shift could leave public police with only "macro-security" claims (Ericson and Haggerty 1997, 29–30) and performing nonprofitable functions.

Many modes may provide security, but as long as the criminal law holds sway as the primary regulatory mode, it can be seen as another means to manage risk: the criminal law "must therefore 'obey' the risk communication rules, formats and technologies of other institutions. The result is a shift in the goals, principles and procedures of criminal law, in the basis of compliance based law enforcement and actuarial justice" (Ericson and Haggerty 1997, 52). The aim of risk-oriented policing is to document the workings of risk management via actuarial systems (Feeley and Simon, 1994), rather than to ensure morality, control crime, or enforce laws.

The symbolic resources of policing, representing the state at its best — its justice, equal treatment of all citizens, and concern for their well-being — are consistently underplayed as resources by the police themselves as well as by the public. Legitimate violence, the law, and public trust sustain policing as a practice. By defining the police instrumentally as the source of law and order, by urging draconian punishments, more prisons, and expansion of the criminal law to cover every aspect of life, and by applying crude economics to public service (both service given and the meaning of being a public servant), the police underestimate their more subtle resources. This narrowing of the mandate is complemented by the diminution and commodification of even sacred symbols.[29] Without those, policing is reduced to the use of force and fraud.

My point is that the seven fundamental issues in evaluating and assessing policing outlined in the previous section, on balance favor the continued muddling through of public policing, balancing routines with emergencies, and sustaining still those odd values that even in diversity are essential — justice, equity, responsibility, and accountability. I do not think that intellectuals' rethinking of these ideas is a solution; praxis has its own rationales and dynamics.

❑ COMMENT

Many of the key questions about the relative social value of types of social control (Silbey 1997) and policing cannot be answered now. I have expressed a preference. Perhaps these questions will form a dialogue about the proper policing discourse so brilliantly evoked in Shearing's description of policing as "a dark glass through which we may catch glimpses of the world which we are tumbling toward" (1992, 426–27). He continues to suggest that this world will be shaped not only by markets but by the sensibilities of people acting within tiny theaters, voicing political views, and representing to themselves and others visions of the future of (police) control.

A dramaturgical perspective focuses on the performance of symbolic actions and the strategies and tactics that characterize interactions. If actions are reduced to economic and or cynical self-serving motives, as Parsons pointed out (1936), we are creating a context where altruism, duty, loyalty, and even sacrifice are merely empty echoes of the past, and where self-serving is the rule, even for those who ostensibly serve others. When the moral and social obligations of policing become externalities; when accountability is a story told externally and internally to manage politics (Moore 1995, 213), and when "preserve and protect" means contributing to a vast, violent wasteland in inner cities, to the world's largest prison population, and to a destroyed segment of minority youth, then market forces have indeed succeeded in shaping not only our vision but our realities.

NOTES

1. Shearing (1992) shows that this context is a Theoretical debate that reflects trends within postmodern, pluralistic societies with decentralized ordering and fragmented authority. It is not databased, nor derived from empirical research designed to assess the relative value of forms of policing for regulating or enhancing given social structures and processes. Police reform must pose analogous questions about the balance between these forms (Brogdan and Shearing 1993).

2. This analysis considers the relationships between types of police with reference to the patterning of transactions and the fit between "policing" and "society" (see Bayley 1969, 1975, 1979, 1985, 1992b, 1994; Reiss 1992b). Little space is given to hybrid or regulatory police (Johnston 1992, 116–17), the growing literature on voluntary and citizen participation in policing, and self-help (Black 1983). Space limitations restrict my comments on these topics.

3. Unfortunately, private policing has few ethnographies (Goodhall 1989) and no ethnographic classics to compare with Westley's Violence and the Police (1977), Rubinstein's brilliant City Police (1972), or James Q. Wilson's pioneering organizational analysis, Varieties of Police Behavior (1968); the studies of Banton (1964), Cain (1973), Holdaway (1983), Smith (1986), Chatterton (1987), Chatterton and Whitehead (1997), and Fielding (1988, 1996) of English policing; Ericson and colleagues on Canadian policing (1981, 1982, 1997), Punch (1979) on Dutch officers, or Van Maanen on American patrol officers (1974).

4. Reports of private research organizations, the Rand Report (Kalakik and Wildhorn 1972) and the Hallcrest, Report (Cunningham and Taylor 1985), are policy-oriented and highly optimistic assessments of the current and future prospects of private policing. Nalla and Newman (1993) chart the ground well. Three excellent general books, Draper (1979), South (1988), and Johnston (1992), and edited collections by Shearing and Stenning (1987) and Matthews (1989) take up general questions and urge careful empirical research on costs (Draper 1979; 62), regulation and accountability (Draper 1979, 24); the dynamics of the relationships between public and private police services (South 1988, 98–99; Shearing 1992, 430–26; Jones and Newburn 1998), and key definitions (Shearing 1992, 399–401). Private policing is also seen as regulation (Shearing and Stenning 1987), private investigation (Goodhall 1989; Morn 1992), corporate security (Atkinson Report 1992), the employment of public police by private corporations (Reiss 1988), and the emergent field of transnational policing (Scheptycki, 1996, forthcoming). Many texts, varying from "how to do it" to "how it was done," guide the development and implementation of security programs (e.g., Timm and Christian 1992). They tend to be proscriptive and hortatory, and to avoid the abiding issues, tensions, and paradoxes of private security work.

5. The study of policing has a history of assumptions (Manning 1997; Johnston 1992, 24–44). The study of the pattern of development, or the "evolution" of policing, has been dominated by explanations of the rise of the public police without sufficient attention to the persistence of informal and quasi-formal modes of control and of self-help (Radzinowicz 1968 does entertain the conflux of the types, however). This focus has blinded many observers to the richness and complexity of policing.

6. As Black (1984) convincingly argues, social control is a dependent variable that reflects, among other things, the degree of social and cultural differentiation in a society. It is as important to identify the causes of policing as a social form as to discover and describe specific consequences of policing "on the ground."

7. The overlapping, contradictory, and paradoxical application any and all of these styles by many agencies, especially those other than the penal style, is a feature of modern America.

8. Clearly, either prevention or deterrence requires developed primary, secondary, or tertiary strategies (Reiss 1995).

9. The role of technology in policing is discussed in P. K. Manning 1992 and 1997, 102–4.

10. The ratio of officers to citizens in urban areas has increased, as has the volume of incidents processed, including crimes (Mastrofski 1990).

11. Studies of police practice and workload studies suggest that the primary function (in times terms) of the police is not crime control as measured in stops, arrests, clearances, and the like, but providing diverse services (see Goldstein 1990, ch. 2).

12. See an interview with Daryl Gates in *Playboy* (fall 1991); a long feature story about Gates in *Vanity Fair* in (August 1991), and a two-part series on the LAPD in the *New York Review of Books* written by John Gregory Donne, in October 1991.

Chief Elizabeth Watson of Houston was the subject of a long C-SPAN interview reshown during the summer of 1991. A PBS television feature in 1990, "Police Chiefs," profiled Chief Daryl Gates of Los Angeles, Anthony Bouza, former chief of police in Minneapolis, and Lee Brown, commissioner of police in New York City.

13. Ms. Was is a black woman beaten by 2 white women in Detroit. They were not arrested, and the mayor (Coleman Young) examined video tapes and urged arrest and prosecution of the 2 white women. They were not arrested. Was, initially charged with robbery, was not taken to court.

14. See Surette 1991 and Ericson 1989, 1991.

15. It nearly impossible to assess the increases in the volume of reported crimes that better technology, access to and number of telephones, and better record-keeping systems have produced, or the decrease in officially recorded calls resulting from community policing tactics such as neighborhood and foot patrol officers, ministations, and voice mail systems, prioritizing calls for service and developing alternative modes of response.

A close examination of CAD, or computer-assisted dispatching, illustrates the complex impacts of new information technology. Calls are more efficiently screened using centralized call collection based on a 3-digit number such as 911 and enhanced 911 that enables call tracing and display of the address of the caller; CAD and associated techniques such as management information systems and computerized record systems shorten pass-through time and ease record-keeping. The mobile digital terminal combines voices, written display, and phone and network capacity to other computer systems. With a computer-based information system, networking — creating interfaces with other systems — is possible. Networking permits police departments to exchange information among themselves as well to access the FBI's National Crime Information Center (NCIC) (Tien and Colton, 1979; Stevens 1989; Geller and Morris 1992).

16. 16. See histories of police reform: Lane 1967; Fogelson 1977; Reppetto 1978; and Bittner 1990.

17. There are very few studies of command and only a few case studies of police departments that address the interaction of command decision making, the politics of the city, and law enforcement (see Hunt and Magenau 1993; Scheingold 1984, 1991; Guyot 1991; and Jackall 1997). Reiner's *Chief Constables* (1991) provides a useful perspective on these issues by chiefs in England, as well as fascinating biographical and career details.

18. The value of applying TQM was summarized well by Gary Sykes, a leading advocate of TQM in policing: "We need to change the business they're in [the police] and change the way they do business" (Sykes 1995).

19. Secret funds are a risky category. Ex-Chief William Hart of the Detroit Police Department was convicted of embezzlement (misuse of a secret fund) and sent to federal prison in 1990.

20. Well-developed case studies, such as those used in business schools, could sharpen our analytic tools. Case studies are useful, as Johnston shows in his analysis of the privatization of policing during the period of the British Thatcher government (1979–92), because they illuminate the complexity of development and privatization as a process. Case studies, for example, suggest not only variations in the quality and kinds of services offered but also the rather less patterned, decentralized changes in American policing. They could illuminate dramatically the looseness of the terms "private" and "privatization."

21. Some forms of indigenous policing — such as tribal police — do not exist in the United Kingdom, while some English elaborations — hybrids, like the railway police and the nuclear transport police, that are between governmental and private — are uniquely British. In international or transnational policing outside the Anglo-American policing world, even more anomalies arise because the connection among law, authority, and territory is broken at least stretched to its limits.

22. The privatization of the prison service was discussed by the English Conservative government in the mid-1990s but was not enacted. Forst, in part 1, discusses the extent of contract prison governance.

23. Provision of these functions as shifting between in-house people in corporations and outsourcing. The downsizing and deskilling of corporate security threatens to be extreme in the coming years. As functions expand, something that might be expected with the growth of community policing, police may continue to pass some functions along to private agencies. These could include activities both inside the criminal justice system and outside it (e.g., licensing of taverns, regulation of traffic, and animal and noise control).

24. Spending some time in the chief's office or as a part of his or her core staff is usually essential for those aspiring to a top command career. The most famous career move of this kind was Daryl Gates's rise to Chief of the Los Angeles Police Department from his earlier position as a driver for Chief William Parker (1950–66). Gates served as chief from 1978 to 1993.

25. These issues are also raised in suits against police departments by women who feel the police failed to protect them, in the face of known threats to their lives, and who want legal remedies in the form of special protection, indemnification, or financial compensation.

26. Studies of the distribution of police services suggest that on the whole, police do not discriminate in reactive services, as measured by response time or time spent in response to calls (Shearing 1984). However, as Black (1983) shows, the character of these activities varies by class. Middle-class people are more likely to be victims, witnesses to crimes, or complainants, while lower-class people are more likely to be suspects.

27. The very optimistic predictions for growth in employment in security published in the Hallcrest Report (Cunningham and Taylor 1985), even based on flawed data and changes in the composition of the labor force in security, have not resulted. In fact, there are indications that private security is being downsized or right-sized in corporations, outsourcing of many functions is proceeding, and some degree of de-skilling may be taking place at the guard level. The growth of electronic surveillance has perhaps reduced the demand for professional in watch-manlike positions. The idea that private policing is thriving is restricted to some sectors within security. The growth may be in deskilled, low-salaried workers. Wage competition plus an expansion in functions could in turn depress the salaries of the public police. Policing is not a binary matter in which growth in "private" policing growth in public policing inhibits. There is an interaction effect and some interdependence of growth.

28. See Bayley 1994, 36–55.

29. The process of expanding and perhaps tarnishing the symbols of state authority, even faux versions of them, is ongoing. Used police cars are used by seniors to patrol disabled parking spots; private security companies create uniforms, decorations, equipment, and vehicle coloration that simulate the image of public police; hats, T-shirts, sweatshirts, and other souvenirs emblazoned with "FBI," "RCMP," and "Michigan State Police" are sold and worn everywhere by anybody; private security guards with virtually no training or supervision carry weapons and use them with impunity on the job; and police and the FBI sell information to private security companies. All such symbolic displays demean the integral of sign vehicles that convey or communicate governmental authority to the public, sustain trust, facilitate legitimacy, and ultimately renew and reward compliance.

PART THREE

Reflections

Comment: Response

Brian Forst

❏ INTRODUCTION

For years I have been strongly attracted to two elements of Peter Manning's work: its extreme thoughtfulness and its unconventionality. He draws lines outside our usual frames of reference; he takes us to notions that no other major authority on policing entertains. It has been said that an overlooked characteristic of fish is that there is no evidence that they are aware of the concept "water." Peter makes us fish aware of water.

Peter's contributions to our thinking about the privatization of policing, like his writings about other aspects of policing, are significant for drawing our attention to overlooked essentials. His reflective work reminds us that much of what we take as truths and givens, the foundations of many of our strongly held positions, are really constructs of the mind, conveniences for thinking about issues like privatization that bring along the risk of reification. In building our models and concepts for analysis we may even end up making them more important than the things and critical issues they represent.

As in his prior writings, Peter focuses the current work on the intangible and social nature of police work: its unpredictability and quaintness, its dependency on skills of persuasion and guile, its dependency on public trust, its reliance on symbols to motivate behavior. To reduce all aspects of police accountability to such measures as crime and arrest rates is to guarantee that the essential intangibles will be neglected, which may ultimately diminish the capacity of the police to control crime and contribute to the preservation of peace and order.

To deal with privatization, Peter abandons the occupational culture perspective used in some of his earlier work in favor of a more phenomenological analysis, a "dramaturgical-theatrical" perspective. This framework allows Peter to see the police, both public and private, as a formal authority operating in "big and little theaters" that act to maintain the vertical order in society, the symbolic hierarchy of worth. The dramaturgical perspective induces a closer focus on aspects of both policing and private security that emphasize credibility based on appearances, images, and impressions. It highlights the dilemma represented by media-driven spectacles such as the Polly Klaas case, which build public trust in policing while consuming disproportionate police resources. His analysis was supported with interviews of directors of corporate security, interviews that reveal the central role of loyalty and trust in different contexts.

Peter sees the rhetoric of managerial economics contributing inordinately both to the decline of public policing and to privatization. His concern is about the problems that arise "when ideologically driven imagery outstrips established institutional functioning," with parallel problems that have arisen in domains outside policing, including higher education and government: "The urgent point is that the [appropriate] language and framework for the debate is not economics and the rhetoric of economics, but the language of social control, illuminated by metaphor." He sees a decline in the rights of employees as but one important undesirable side effect of the shift from public to private policing.

Peter reserves his sharpest laser beam strikes for the Total Quality Management (TQM) movement, popular among a large and growing number of police executives. He notes that TQM is especially dangerous as it applies to core police work, involving conflict and dispute, particularly in complex metropolitan police departments. He deconstructs TQM, revealing superficialities and ironies in some of its applications to policing, especially its tendency to shift power from street cops to command management. He raises fundamental, critical questions about the appropriateness of increasingly popular strategies that emphasize service to individual consumers, common not just to TQM but to larger community-oriented strategies of policing as well: Is such strategy fully compatible with the basic mandate of police to serve the state through democratically elected representatives? Are members of the general public equipped to judge the competence of police? What risks are involved?

❏ POINTS OF AGREEMENT

Peter and I agree on many issues. Although his descriptions and definitions tend to be more elaborate than mine, we use essentially the same definitions of privatization and policing, relying heavily on critical distinctions made by Egon Bittner (1970). We both see the basic question as this: How shall the public best be policed? We both see serious flaws in public policing and in the private security sector. We agree that the police are losing their monopoly of legitimate violence, a trend that has a variety of historical precedents. We agree that the paramilitary imagery of the professional policing model has hurt policing, and that techniques derived from economic principles are often misused in assessing public policy generally and police performance in particular, especially under the powerful influence of anti-intellectual populism. We both see the public poorly served by media that play to public fears about crime, especially in light of basic questions about whether the police should be responsible for just crime and order maintenance, or public safety generally, or perhaps even matters related to larger quality-of-life considerations. We agree that more research is needed to examine the full effects of the privatization of policing on both the level and distribution of policing services throughout various sectors of society.

Of particular importance, Peter and I agree that concerns about efficiency must be tempered by concerns about equity and justice, that attempts to reform policing must be mindful of the demands made on police dealing with human misery and despair. We are both keenly interested in the question: What is it that motivates police?

More fundamentally, we both aim to *describe* and to *assess,* in order to provide an informed basis for thinking about policing not only as a subject of scholarly inquiry but as an activity about which policies are contemplated, created, modified, enforced, and terminated. How Peter and I, and others, think about policing determines not only our descriptions and assessments but also any positions we may hold about how policing should be changed.

❏ METAPHORS, MODELS, AND VERITIES

Peter's descriptions and assessments of policing, while similar to mine in many respects, depart at several junctures. Let us first consider descriptive issues, then differences in our respective assessments.

Peter and I are both deeply concerned about the decline of such virtues as honor, duty, loyalty, and trust. We are not of one mind, however, on the primary sources of this decline. Peter attributes the decline principally to a constellation of issues related to "economistic" thinking: metaphoric images based on theories of free markets, preoccupation with illusory measures of efficiency and effectiveness in assessing performance and with the jargon of business management to alter systems of accountability — all at the expense of more fundamental elements of human activity. I see the decline of basic human virtues related no less to other factors: the growth of freedom and leisure without enlightenment, the absence of major societal crisis such as war to bind people, cynicism bred by media obsessed with the imperfections of well-known people and institutions and often conspicuously uninterested in their contributions, the glorification of self-indulgent behaviors, and the atomization of family and community bonds.

Our market economy certainly serves as an accomplice, providing avenues that expedite the subordination of duty and self-control to less noble qualities, and facilitating the substitution of parental involvement in the raising of children with television and other electronic media. The research of others, in any case, suggests that the market economy is not the sole driving force here. Amitai Etzioni (1993) sees the problem as one of excessive concern about rights and too little about responsibilities, which suggests roots in freedom. He attributes the decline of moral behavior to materialism, to be sure, but as well to the fall of family, decline of work ethic, bombardment of corrupting media messages, and a weakened willingness of public and private institutions to instill a moral sense in individuals. Francis Fukuyama (1995) surveys the dominant nation-cultures of the world to unearth the primary sources of trust, or "social capital," and concludes that the highest levels of trust are to be found in countries with strong market economies — Japan, Germany, Holland, Switzerland, and the United States (except for the inner cities) — while low levels persist in Russia, China, southern Italy, and France. James Q. Wilson (1993) finds the moral sense to be an innate human attribute, one that we are drawn away from by the influence of existential philosophers, moral relativists, and Freudian psychologists. Etzioni identifies materialism and Wilson mentions radical free market economic thinking as contributors to the mix of factors behind the decline of moral behavior, but none of these observers place the bulk of the burden of the decline on our economic system. And few scholars report lower levels of duty, loyalty, and trust in private settings than in public ones generally.

Early on in his essay. Peter assigns the burden of guilt for the decline of these qualities to the ideology of our economic system. He observes that the complex relations between public and private police are set in the context of democratic capitalism with market economies and this alone is a force that shapes organizational niches, strategies, and patterns of competition.

Peter caricatures contemporary economics — for its unrealistic assumptions, for its failure to include critical inputs in its prescriptive applications, and for its failure to consider long-term factors. Economists have offered responses to each of these criticisms, some more satisfactory than others.[1] Peter's criticisms echo a long tradition of legitimate lampooning of the field of economics by other social scientists, especially for its support of work that has relied excessively on notions of rational behavior, notions that have been shown by systematic observation to be a poor basis for models of most violent crimes, crimes of passion, crimes induced by alcohol, and juvenile delinquency. Yet the field of economics has itself produced some of the most penetrating criticisms of theories that do not venture beyond conventional neoclassical assumptions of rational behavior, near-perfect information, search costs, and human capital. Recent writings by Hirschman, Phillips, Frank, and Akerlof and Yellin provide examples that are especially pertinent here.

Albert Hirschman's (1986) identification of metapreferences represents a sharp departure from the standard neoclassical assumption that tastes are given, a departure that bolsters Hirschman's influential (1979) exit-voice-loyalty model. Llad Phillips (1993) uses Hirschman's work, along with that of sociologist Jack Katz (1988), to augment the neoclassical model of crime and justice, and the deterrence model in particular, with notions of moral suasion and loyalty. Phillips concludes that the neoclassical model is useful but limited, that more encompassing — not different — frameworks provide richer insights into human behavior and public policy.

Robert Frank (1988), borrowing from Adam Smith's ([1759] 1966) theory of moral sentiments, observes that commitments and altruistic behaviors are more effectively conveyed by emotions such as anger, envy, love, and shame than by reasoned argument, that these are more fundamentally moral sentiments than they are strategic weapons. Frank's reward theory of behavior argues that combining moral sentiments with other incentive systems, such as contracts and pay levels, can provide a stronger principal-agent relationship than either alone.

George Akerlof and Janet Yellin (1994, 173–209) combine elements of Frank's work with those of Hirschman's to focus on the role of community values and loyalties in controlling crime. They build on the neoclassical model by observing that high crime rates desensitize members of the community to intolerance of crime, while police misbehavior and insensitivity to inner-city problems and overly punitive sanctions shift community support from the legitimate authorities to neighborhood gangs, which provide an alternative form of territorial protection. Akerlof and Yellin provide a coherent utilitarian theory for community policing, which has been largely absent from the criminological literature on the subject.

Peter makes a much simpler distinction about economic thinking. The high road of economics is represented in Paul Samuelson's (1947, 1954) research, suggesting that policing is a collective good.[2] The low road is reflected in the more recent "economistic" work that treats policing as a "competitive, services-producing" activity, a faddish, ideologically driven, and specious construct of the Reagan-Bush years.

A more useful distinction might be made between the discipline and the ideologies of economics. Large organizations, public or private, might indeed be foolish for hiring economists and efficiency experts, either on a full-time or consultative basis, to assist in applying models from economics to support decisions and policies that revolve primarily around ethical issues. Those that choose to ignore such counsel for other matters, however, do so at their own peril.

Peter's thesis on economic imperialism recalls Lord Keynes's (1973) famous maxim: "Practical men, who believe themselves to be quite exempt from any intellectual influences, are usually the slaves of some defunct economist" (p. 383). As far as I can tell, police executives are more the slaves of city budgets, police unions, reporters, and prosecutors than they are of the work of economists. They are not so much subjected to bad economics as they are to little or no economic thinking at all. The police executives I know are much more likely to have taken degrees in psychology than in economics.[3]

Of particular interest is Peter's placement of issues related to resource allocation and performance in the domain of rhetoric and metaphor while loyalty, violence, and other issues related to the sacred craft of the good street cop are placed in the domain of things real. Thus, such terms as "service," "efficiency," and "effectiveness" are economistic, relegated to quotation marks, while the vital issues of policing — social control, trust, and craft — are not.[4] The problem of rationing scarce patrol officer time effectively across competing demands is more rhetorical than real: "The officer's role as envisioned by economic rhetoric is to serve as a demand manager." Economic constructs aren't just figments of the imagination; they're ignoble: "Lurking in the background is the fee-for-service model that is the theoretical basis for market transactions."

Others have legitimately questioned the isolation of patrol officers from the public without placing the lion's share of the blame for that isolation on contemporary economics and the scientific management reform movement. A long line of policing scholars from Bittner (1970) and Klockars (1985) to Skolnick and Fyfe have (1993) chronicled the use of military metaphors to justify a particular brand of professionalism in policing promoted by O. W. Wilson, J. Edgar Hoover, William Parker, and others. That model surely contributed more substantially to the alienation of police from urban communities than did concepts from managerial economics.

Understating the importance of other influences that appear to have been more devastating to policing than that of economics and management science is but one of at least two serious problems with the attribution noted above. Another is the proverbial problem of throwing out baby with the bathwater. In essentially the same way that much, perhaps most, but not all about professionalism and loyalty is really *good for* policing, so is much, perhaps most, but not all about economics and management science good for policing. Peter sees "third-rate economics applied to policing" as more influential than, say, third-rate sociology or third-rate public administration and so, evidently, more deserving of criticism, yet he suggests that any economic thinking other than that dealing with collective goods is inapplicable to policing and third-rate.

Let us turn now to differences in our assessments about policing and privatization. Peter's assessments depart most sharply from mine on the matter of whether questions of policy — issues of resource allocation — should be assessed on the basis of measurements of effectiveness and efficiency. We can approach this issue by reconsidering the question, What is it that motivates police? Peter and I agree that the patrol officer trying to exercise discretion wisely is not likely to be motivated solely by grand statements about the goal of crime control, any more than a teacher trying to organize a lesson plan for the next day is going to be motivated by concerns about deficiencies in the performance of U.S. students compared with that of students in Japan or Germany. Peter's thinking departs from mine regarding where we go from there: he focuses on the power of symbols — "sacred traditions and practices, craft-based work, and mystification and ideology" — and I am more interested in the linkages between the goal of crime control and incentive systems that motivate the officer to operate in a manner that actually reduces crime. I am more persuaded than he that accountability systems can be devised that create incentives for officers to be more effective in responding to crimes so that they can be solved, and more effective in working with private citizens, commercial establishments, private security personnel and others both to prevent and solve crimes.

These systems should be, and are, based no less on factors reflecting *process* — lapses in the conduct of duty, citizen complaints about rudeness and other forms of misconduct, excessive use of leave, and so on — than on crime rate measures, over which the police have limited control. The systems should be designed especially to deal with long-standing concerns of inner-city residents: lack of responsiveness, lack of civility, and other revelations of lack of respectful service.

Such systems of accountability can and should make use of symbols to motivate appropriate behavior: formal awards and letters of commendation, informal acknowledgments, improved assignments, bonus leave time, and so on. But the symbols, in the manner of "carrots" that encourage effective and virtuous behaviors and "sticks" that discourage ineffective and harmful behaviors, must be purposefully allocated within a framework for assessing performance. If TQM offers an effective framework for improving police performance and efficiency, with a minimum of undesirable side effects, then two cheers for TQM. If a better framework can be found, three cheers for it.

Peter is especially critical of efforts to make police operations more efficient, to reduce costs, noting difficulties of doing so without further rationing services. Yet in the District of Columbia, the Metropolitan Police Department has demonstrated a perverse ability to simultaneously increase costs *and* reduce services — through malingering, excessive overtime charges, and other wasteful practices. It may be only a coincidence that the decline has been especially sharp since 1985, when the department stopped evaluating the performance of officers (Powell et al. 1997, A 20). Levels of efficiency appear to vary substantially both among police departments and over time within given departments, and they are not beyond the grasp of police administrators to control through a system of institutional rewards and sanctions, and using good, old-fashioned leadership.

Attempts to increase efficiency can be, and have been, counterproductive if poorly administered, but that does not invalidate efficiency as a legitimate goal of policing. Efficiency is important as a first order of police business because budget constraints are real, not metaphorical. A more efficient police department is one that can deliver more of the vital police services — maintaining the peace and reducing human misery — that both Peter and I care about, given those palpable constraints.

Emphasis on efficiency in the control of crime by police departments may also tend to countervail against the regressive distributional effects of privatization, especially in urban areas. Crime victims are disproportionately poor. Shifts away from an emphasis on efficiency in crime control, away from focus on crime hot spots to anything else, could tend to have negative consequences for the poorest, least powerful strata of our society. To deemphasize efficiency on behalf of the poor could prove to be more tragic than ironic.

The dramaturgical conception of policing — "to take on the central shaping role of the media in creating and constructing meanings, experience, and memories" — is interesting and potentially useful, but we need to learn more about how it can be used to inform the administration of a police department. How does a chief do this in a way that takes into account (1) the full implications of any particular set of meanings, selection of experiences, and memories, (2) the effects on the behaviors of patrol officers, detectives, mid-level managers, police executives, and support personnel, (3) other public officials, (4) victims, offenders, bystanders and (5) the vast array of private security personnel? If the dramaturgical perspective is to provide a really useful basis for thinking about policing, we will have to be more explicit about it.

To be fair, we must recognize that the potential power of the dramaturgical perspective for informing and improving policing, like that of other perspectives, must carry along its own set of risks. How can we ensure that that perspective is not trivialized and misused in the sorts of ways that legitimate constructs of economics have been trivialized and misused? Loyalty, for example, is very much a two-edged sword: virtuous and useful when found in effective organizations working to achieve worthy ends, but a force of evil when used in support of nefarious schemes, people, and institutions. Any attempt to make the dramaturgical perspective more explicit is bound to run such risks, yet to avoid such attempts may be to keep the perspective relegated to the lofty tower of potentially useful ideas.

Regardless of whether the dramaturgical perspective does or does not play a role in thinking about and assessing policing, performance assessment systems are here to stay, objections notwithstanding. Many of my colleagues in the academy have come to despise, with strong and legitimate reasons, the heavy reliance on student evaluations to provide a basis for assessing teaching effectiveness. The evaluations induce pandering, the substitution of entertainment for serious learning, grade inflation, and a variety of related sins. Most universities have nonetheless been unable to put in place superior alternatives for making those assessments in support of merit review, tenure, and promotion decisions. With similarly compelling reasons we can bemoan the use of crime counts to provide a basis for assessing the effectiveness of the police in controlling crime; we can further lament the use of crime control as an overarching goal of policing; and we can wish to replace accountability systems altogether with integrity and trust. But until we find ways of improving those systems, we have little choice but to make the most of the existing flawed alternatives.

Of course, we can find ways to improve our systems of accountability. A few universities are augmenting student evaluations with other inputs: peer reviews, analyses of course syllabi, teaching portfolios, and so on. Similarly, police performance assessments can augment insufficient measures and replace erroneous ones with valid surveys of citizens, rigorous analyses of data on calls for service and the dispatch of patrol units, citizen complaints, and other valid indicators of performance.

In the meantime, dramatic declines in homicides in New York, Boston, and elsewhere during the 1990s following the strengthening of accountability systems more explicitly related to crime and order maintenance suggest that those systems may not be all bad. We cannot know that these accountability systems are truly effective until we design research projects that measure the relationships more systematically at two levels: (1) between the larger crime-control and order-maintenance objectives and the incentives implemented, and (2) between the incentives and actual police behaviors.

☐ CONCLUSION

René Dubos (1968) has observed that utilitarian considerations need not conflict with more noble ones: "The Brooklyn Bridge . . . demonstrated that steel and concrete could serve for the creation of meaningful beauty; through it, technology in the service of a purpose became a joy and inspiration for painters and poets" (p. 196). The design of that structure satisfied basic concerns of efficiency and effectiveness, and did so without any loss of more elusive measures of quality and craft. Similarly, at a time of flagrant free-agency excesses in professional athletics, the legendary performances of basketball's Michael Jordan and baseball's Cal Ripken, as reflected in their respective measures of effectiveness and efficiency, do not come at the expense of their revealed loyalty to the Chicago Bulls and Baltimore Orioles, respectively. Though these are all exceptional cases, it should be clear that concerns about effectiveness and efficiency need not interfere with Dubos's noble "pursuit of significance" (1968, 150–215).

Today's most burning question confronting public safety in the United States is not primarily about the fine points of performance measurement, or about how much privatization is the right amount. It is about how to organize our vast variety of human and nonhuman resources to restore public safety in our poorest and most crime-prone areas. Scholars can help by providing more thorough assessments of how alternative systems of accountability, both formal and informal, that aim to improve efficiency, effectiveness, and integrity actually enhance the ability of police to accomplish their primary mission, to serve and protect the public. No single perspective alone, utilitarian or dramaturgical, is likely to suffice.

NOTES

1. Friedman (1953) has argued that models, economic and otherwise, should be assessed not on the basis of the realism of their assumptions, but on the basis of the accuracy of their predictions. Peter's criticism of the failure of the Atkinson Security Project model to include intangibles such as loyalty and morale speaks to the difficulty of assessing the value of such intangibles; assuming them to be zero by ignoring them altogether may indeed be worse than imputing an arbitrarily high value. Zero imputation is consistent with generally accepted accounting principles for assessing "goodwill" and other intangibles, but economists tend to prefer the assessments of such intangibles as revealed by market transactions. Long-term factors are in fact included in the Atkinson model under the user's choice of either the net present value or the internal rate of return construct.

2. Samuelson's core contribution to the literature on collective goods, although concentrated in a three-page 1954 article, "The Pure Theory of Public Expenditure," is substantial in that it derives conditions for optimal resource allocation in an economy in which there are two types of goods, private and public. Samuelson defines a collective good as one for which "each individual's consumption leads to no subtraction from any other individual's consumption of that good" (p. 386). The article is significant largely for having launched a small library of literature on collective choice. A summary of this literature is in Mueller (1989). Economists generally agree that defense and courts are "pure" public goods, in which the consumption benefits of any individual do not depend on the benefits received by others. Beyond those two examples, there has been considerable disarray over which publicly provided goods and services qualify as pure public goods. Core functions of law enforcement clearly qualify as a public good, but practical implications for policing policy are unclear. Samuelson's landmark 1954 article makes no explicit reference to policing.

3. Peter observes that police often take degrees in sociology, criminal justice, psychology, and political science.

4. Peter's treatment of economic considerations is reminiscent of a 1997 *New Yorker* essay on drivel by Steve Martin: "She had painted a tabletop still-life — a conceptual work, in that it had no concept. Thus the viewer became a "viewer," and looked at a painting, which became a "painting." The "viewer" then left the museum to "discuss" the experience with "others."

Comment: Response

Peter K. Manning

I am pleased to respond to Brian Forst's comments on my portion of our book, his analysis, observations about perspective and theorizing, and his vision for the future. His trenchant and thoughtful remarks not only deserve response and appreciation, but have stimulated rethinking of some of my reservations and criticisms.

Since this is a dialogue with a profoundly moral edge, it is not surprising perhaps that we acknowledge the context as a set of fuzzy concepts — justice, equity, quality of life and services; trust, loyalty, and duty. These rather quaint ideas, as he points out, have been seen as economic notions and the organizing themes of welfare economics. Brian Forst's rather stark summary remark concluding his comment is worthy and evocative — the issue is "how to organize our vast variety of human and nonhuman resources to restore public safety in our poorest and most crime-prone areas." There we begin.

I wish to elaborate some points about economics, drama, research, and the future as well as to return to the issue of privatization.

☐ ECONOMICS AND DRAMA

The discipline of economics, and perhaps psychology, is the only social *science* we possess; its practitioners have received many well-deserved Nobel prizes, and the "trickle down" effects have been salutary in political science, anthropology, and sociology. Rational-choice theories have well eroded our once-holophrastic disciplines. Economic models, theorizing, and data analysis techniques dominate the core social science journals.

The damage done by, with, and in the name of economics, in my overstated, sometimes unfair critique, occasionally issues from economists. More often, in my view, it emanates from others, those C. Wright Mills (1960) calls the "wholesalers" and "retailers" of ideas. These are not creators and paradigm shapers. My concern is with those who translate, transform, package, and put the right spin or take on very complex ideas from the social sciences and urge their implementation in civic administration and government more generally.

The science of forensics, public administration, law, and even sociology shaped the first police reform movements, and the reformers — August Vollmer, Bruce Smith, O. W. Wilson, and William Parker (even granting his excesses) — practiced their crafts even as they reshaped the future of policing. The present reformers do not practice policing and, as Brian Forst points out, they are not trained in economics. Police chiefs today, covertly wedded to crime-control rhetoric, in part to curry favor with the dominant patrol officer segment, speak of community policing and assemble *SWAT* teams and other paramilitary units (Kraska and Kappeler, 1997) while seeking to convince the public that something other than policing as usual — "community policing," — is under way.

Policing is vulnerable in many respects. Although a conservative organization and occupation, it is subject to trends and fads in public discourse and is influenced by the halo effect of prestigious academics and consultants and the initiatives of government funding agencies. The influence of economics, cost-benefit and impact analysis, TQM, and other management techniques (like zero-base budgeting, management by objectives, and quality circles), is vulgarized by public gurus. Brian Forst correctly penetrates my caricature, underscoring the abiding and more important question of the quality of policing and its moral, interactional, and symbolic context. He is quite right to assert the utility of economic thinking for analysis, understanding, and reform in organizations that produce a product in a market.

The drama of little and big theaters is a play on an uneasy alliance — a collage of the ideas of Goffman, Burke, and Foucault. (I suspect that during one of his visits to Berkeley Foucault might have met Goffman. I hope so.) Once this perspective is adopted to clarify the mirage of politics, organizational strategies, and tactics, to see how performances, "self-presentations" (organizations seen as actors), especially in a dance with the mass media, surface, the moral thrust of any dramaturgical analysis remains rather ambiguous. The extant criticism of Goffman's work, save that of Phillip Manning (1993), is replete — I should say redolent — with tenacious criticisms of its intended morality. The moral thrust remains: what is unsaid about performances that produce working consensus, truths that are believed lies, surfaces that unite, teams that are situated fragile coalitions, and moral values and selves that live in the cracks of institutions and backstage. This perspective reveals, as Goffman (1983b) urged, the vagaries of unexamined power and authority wherever they exist, a point brilliantly explicated in his work on silence (Goffman 1983a), or "the felicity condition," and its tacit role in sustaining meaning. Silence, even the internal dialogue of the self (Wiley 1994), supports unreflective interactions and sustains power. Conversely, conventional exchanges validate the status quo (Bourdieu 1991, 170). Unreflective, mutually reinforcing validation of the organizational mandate feeds into the manipulation of publics, media disingenuousness (if that is possible), bad faith (in the technical sense of acting inauthentically), and substituting spectacles for civilized discourse and debate.

Having said that, it is perfectly true also that reading and applying the maxims of *The Presentation of Self in Everyday Life (Goffman 1959)*, like mining *The Prince,* or *Mein Kampf,* can be equally useful in power seeking and control, whether by police chiefs, fire chiefs, or mayors. We know far too little about this sort of applied postmodern politics. The dramaturgical perspective should reveal the counterpoint and seductive, enduring appeal of modern irrationalities, as do the writings of Isaiah Berlin, Søren Kierkegaard, Jean-Paul Sartre and in recent fiction, such odd companions as James Ellroy, Joyce Carole Oates, Primo Levi, and Kazuo Ishiguro.

❏ RESEARCH THEMES AND LIMITS

As Brian Forst points out, and his work demonstrates, much of the research bearing on the claims of privatization in its various forms (as he well and usefully differentiates them) is unsatisfying. Much remains to be undertaken. We both focus on conceptual distinctions and matrices to outline the relationships requiring clarification. We examine the limits of metaphors and methods, the limited empirical range of studies, their often theoretically impoverished or theory-heavy decadent frameworks, and the abiding "black box" problem. I am most concerned about opening and analyzing the black box. The focus and measurement of inputs and outputs without careful analysis of the interpretive processes by which raw material is transformed into meaningful and valued information leaves the black box as an unseen operator.

We lack useful, clear, penetrating, and time-based comparative research, in my view necessarily ethnographic in some measure, that would enable comparisons of key concepts like violence, fatal force, quality of service, and even such vague notions as cost savings. Since typically both the numerator and the denominator cost-benefits calculations in public administration are estimates or arbitrarily assigned values, results are semiempirical consequences of such assignment. The key ideas, such as the costs of patrol, an arrest, a prevented crime, running a jail, or producing security are unknown hypotheticals. To show that a private company has lower costs than a governmental agency is a meaningless comparison because the basis for the calculations is unrevealed or is a measurement of a narrow aspect of a larger set of functions and tasks. In the absence of a carefully delineated context, studies of privatization remain hanging in social space, and do not describe the context in which decisions, ignorance, politics, interpretations and symbols, are weighed, nor how alternative measurements and assessments are debated. Even such apparently simple matters as the value to society and consequences of overtime pay for police cannot be established outside organizational context (Bayley and Worden, forthcoming). Useful examples of examining context are Brian Forst's work on the quality of arrests in Washington, D.C. (1983) and gun control; Fyfe's (1988) analyses of fatal force, and Reiss's work on police employment (1988).

This review perhaps permits a return to my criticisms of research and polemics advocating privatization. My concern is less about economistic thinking, or misapplied rational choice theory in public administration and government, than about sloppy inferences and indefensible claims drawn from this complex, contradictory set of moot findings and *portmanteau* buzz words. Contrast this with the intellectual content of earlier police reform movements. Police in the late forties and early fifties seized on crime control as a symbolic vehicle for a professionalizing movement directed to winning political power and autonomy. This was linked internally to evaluation and "production," usually indicated by fairly concrete measures of activity such as "clearances" (of reported crimes), arrests, traffic stops and tickets (and later, DWI's), juvenile encounters, and so on. These means-focused measures, like cost savings, beg the question of the context and purpose of such activity, and they are easily reified and mistaken for the purposes of the job. Officers, in turn, call these reports their "cheat sheets" and "lies." These indicators in turn are used by economists and others to characterize police work, and indirect symbolic indicators of process were taken as impact statements.

This rather clever transformation converted quality into quantity, and this remains the ideology of current policing: the "job is on the streets." That is as useful as seeing the work of Toyota Motors, Microsoft, or Royal Dutch Shell as being entirely on the production line. To assess the quality of police service, or performance, to audit in some sensible fashion, creative rethinking of the measures that count, or measuring quality, must be undertaken.[1]

As Brian Forst urges, the central issue is one of equity and quality of service, and linking these matters to accountability internally and externally. Past research is not very helpful in this regard. Most criminal justice research in ahistorical, atheoretical, and ameliorative, a combination destined to produce trivial results. To some degree, we are limited in this quest, because the dispersed, ecologically independent entrepreneurial model of policing conceals the context of patrol work. The high politics of decision making, command practice, and the dilemmas of middle management are virtually unstudied. Unless observers are to be attached to officers and supervisors, the relationship between incentives and actions, choices and policing cannot be accurately described. Furthermore, slickly written and encapsulated case studies which gloss actual outcomes (rather than internal decisions and relationalizations — management), and assert success even though the chief was fired, the data do not support the claims, and the programs were never properly implemented, keep the black box fully closed.

❏ THE FUTURE

The dialectic in police organization is between the occupational cultures or segments within and the rules, procedures, and policies that constrain policing. These include law, standards of practice with respect to the use of violence, and other written directives. From this come the overt dramas of praxis or little theaters. The little theater, the drama of policing, remains a key window into police practice, and by extension, into crime control and quality-of-life indicators that policing can shape. The quality of life is patterned by crime, but in no simple fashion. Here is a sketch.

Policing focuses inordinately its personnel and resources on spaces seen as risky, dangerous, and full of disreputables. This is indicated and seen as true by the history of arrests, seizures, calls, and other official indexes, as well as the oral traditions of patrol officers passed on as common sense. Violence by police and toward police clusters also in these spaces. Victim surveys suggest that even higher rates of victimization exist in these areas than those shown by the Uniform Crime Reporting System. The most serious crimes cluster in these spaces as well. Calls for service are one part easily tracked, but proactive stops, inquiries, interviews, and other interventions are also carried out here and often unremarked or untraceable through records.

This focused activity means that serious crimes and the gratitude that settles on police for their attention to such disruptive acts are in a few known areas of a city. The human losses (deaths, suicides, felonious assaults, and the range of attempted or alleged serious crimes) and their emotional burdens in stress and fear further drain these disorganized areas. The absence of witnesses — family and friends — to the majority of inner-city homicides means that the clearance rate (an organizational fiction in any case) has been falling for more than twenty years, and the potential for gratitude from victim's families has been reduced. The search for witnesses by the police often involves threats, intimidation, deals to facilitate testimony, and — worst of all — counterthreats and killings of witnesses to prevent testimony.[2] As Sherman (1992) shows, arrests, like those for domestic assaults, increase the likelihood of rearrest in inner-city neighborhoods.

Crime control, defined as reactive search for the offender in the interests of punishment, or territorial control using zero-tolerance policies, reduces the thin veneer of trust and reciprocity binding crime-dependent areas with legitimate authority of all kinds. It produces a reverse cycle of exchange — that is, decreasing exchange, a negative reciprocities multiplier. Thus, although whites and middle-class blacks in the suburban rings around cities advocate integration, they support crime-control strategies and rhetoric which target blacks in practice. They urge efficient crime control in the inner cities and quality service in their own territories. (Miller, 1997)

Within police departments I have studied, I have seen little evidence that police are practicing more efficient administration with the possible exception of the Chicago department. (They have financial officers in each precinct with advanced training in business practice and accounting.) I do take the point that policing can combine low quality and high expenditures, but neither can be made meaningful without comparison to some standard. The challenge of community policing is being met by the "road officers." They consider it a misleading farce. Newly hired chiefs in the three cities I know well in the Midwest are publicly taking a very hard-line crime-control stance, in spite of evidence of falling crime rates in all these cities and once-strong community policing programs in two of them.

How does one connect aggressive and punitive crime control strategies, the popularity of community policing, and the rise of paramilitary units across the country in cities of all sizes (Kraska and Kappeler 1997)? Does ths fit the current socioeconomic approach and public language of policing reformers? As Brian Forst notes, research is needed on the connections between incentives and behavior on the one hand, and policies and accountability on the other. Consider the well-publicized crime-control strategies used in New York and credited to Commissioner William Bratton (1994–96) The figures can most likely be explained by three things: (1) manipulation of the crime statistics by the "comstat" sergeants who process by hand crime reports in the precincts, (2) the impact of hiring twelve thousand new officers in the NYPD in the previous two years and deploying them to suppress crime, and (3) the decrease in crime across the country during that same period. Bratton held captains (precinct heads) publicly accountable for crime in their precincts and then allocated personnel using police-saturation tactic. Since there are no independent data by which to validate the NYPD's claims, it is difficult to dismiss the argument that the crime statistics were rigged, in part as a response to public ridicule of the captains by top command and tactical deployment for short-term effects.[3] The zero-tolerance policy, a version of coproduction, shows that policies and personnel (augmented by private finance), can suppress disorder in areas where the middle and working classes confront disorganized urban masses.

This suggests the merits of a final point. Unless and until there is some consensual definition of such matters as crime, crime control, order, and disorder that do not leave them to the unreviewed, backstage, operational decisions of the police, means-oriented measures such as efficiency, and tactics like TQM, research will be of little value. Most departments will change little if at all (recall that the modal size of police departments in America is about fifteen officers). Cost-benefit calculations have no meaningful policy consequences when defined in theory, or by arbitrary conventions, especially in an organization that produces violence, disorder, and chaos as a part of its routine work. Policing rarely has stated policy, goals or objectives. If policing is claimed to produce consensus via value-added activities, by convincing the public that it contributes to public well-being or security, changes in meaning over time, and must combine efficiency with equity (Moore 1995), we return to the fundamental problem of politics, drama and rhetoric.

NOTES

1. I suggested in *Narcs' Game* (1979) weighing seizures and drug types, as well as their market value, against the costs of informant payments, front money, and salaries including overtime to compare the relative effectiveness of drug law enforcement. Arrests are easily generated and have little bearing on use, sales, quality, or quantity of the drugs on the street.

2. See Simon (1992) and Corwin (1996) on the dynamics of homicide investigation in inner-city Baltimore and south-central Los Angeles.

3. Mr. Bratton did not call his approach community policing. He had been hired to demolish community policing after Lee Brown was fired and Rudolph Giuliani won the 1993 mayoral election in New York City.

Bibliography

Akerlof, G., and J. Yellin. 1994. "Gang Behavior, Law Enforcement, and Community Values." In *Values and Public Policy,* edited by H. J. Aaron, T. E. Mann, and T. Taylor. Washington, D.C.: Brookings.

Aristotle. 1943. *Politics.* Modern Library.

"Atkinson Report," 1992, *Security Journal* 3(1), including Duncan, Gale, J. Tofflemire, and R. Yaksick, 2–3; Duncan et al., "Conceptualizing a Value-Added Approach to "The ASIS Foundation Atkinson Security Project" by Security Management: The Atkinson Security Project I," 4–13; Duncan et al., "The Atkinson Value-Added Model: The Atkinson Security Project II," 14–26; Duncan et al., "An Implementation of the Atkinson Model: The Atkinson Security Project III," 27–44; and J. Tofflemire, K. Duncan, and S. Gale, "The ASIS Foundation Benchmark II Survey Study," 45–56.

Altheide, D. 1992. "Gonzo Justice." *Symbolic Interaction,* 15: 69–86.

———. 1997. "The News Media, the Problem Frame, and the Production of Fear." *Sociological Quarterly* 38: 647–68.

Angell, J. 1971. "Toward an Alternative to the Classic Police Organizational Arrangements: A Democratic Model." *Criminology* 9: 185–206.

Audit Commission. 1991–1992 paper 9 [of Local Authorities and the National Health Service]. London: Her Majesty's Stationery Office.

Bacon, S. 1939. "The Early Development of American Municipal Police: A Study in the Evolution of Controls in a Changing Society." Ph.D diss., Yale University.

Banton, M. 1964. *The Policeman in the Community.* New York: Basic Books.

Barley, S. 1986. "Technology as an Occasion for Structuring." *Administrative Science Quarterly* 31: 78–108.

Bayley, D. 1969. *The Police and Politics in India.* Princeton: Princeton University Press.

———. 1975. "The Police in the Political Development of Europe." In *The Formation of Nation Sates in Western Europe,* edited by C. Tilley Princeton: Princeton University Press.

———. 1979. "Police Function, Structure and Control in Western Europe and North America." In *A Review of Research,* edited by N. Morris and M. Tonry *Crime and Justice:* Chicago: University of Chicago Press.

———. 1983. *Encyclopedia of Crime and Justice,* S.V. "police: history."

———. 1985. *Patterns of Policing.* Rutgers, N.J.: Rutgers University Press.

———. 1992a. "Back from the Wonderland, or Toward a Rational Use of Police Resources." Unpublished paper, Centre for Criminology, University of Toronto.

———. 1992b. "Comparative Organization of the Police in the English-Speaking Countries." In. *Modern Policing.* Vol. 15 of *Crime and Justice:* A Review of Research, edited by M. Tonry and N. Moriss Chicago: University of Chicago Press.

———. 1994. The Future of Policing. New York: OUP.

Bayley, D., and C. Shearing. 1996. "The Future of Policing." *Law and Society Review* 30: 585–606.

Bayley, D., and R. Worden. Forthcoming. "Police Use of Overtime." Report to the U.S. Justice Department.

Beck, U. 1992. *Risk Society: Toward a New Modernity.* London: Sage, Ltd.

Becker. D.C. 1995. *The Encyclopedia of Police Science,* 2d ed., S.V. "private security."

Bennet, T. 1990. *Evaluating Neighborhood Watch.* Aldershot, Eng.: Gower.

Benson. B.L. 1998. *To Serve and Protect: Privatization and Community in Criminal Justice.* New York: New York University Press.

Bittner, E 1970. *The Functions of the Police in Modern Society.* Washington, D.C.: National Institute of Mental Health.

———. 1974. "Florence Nightingale in Pursuit of Willie Sutton: A Theory of Police." In *The Potential for Reform of Criminal Justice,* edited by Herbert Jacobs. Beverly Hills: Sage.

———. 1990. *Aspects of Police Work.* Boston: Northeastern University Press.

Black, D. 1976. *The Behavior of Law.* San Diego: Academic Press.

———. 1980. *Manners and Customs of the Police.* New York: Academic Press.

——— 1983. "Crime as Social Control." *American Sociological Review* 48: 34–45.

———, ed. 1984. *Toward a Theory of Social Control.* 2 vol. San Diego: Academic Press.

Boeck, S., and G. Lynn. 1996. "Securing the Olympics" *USA Today,* 17 July.

Bordua, D. 1966. *International Encyclopedia of The Social Sciences,* S.V. "police."

Bordua, D., and E. Haurek. 1971. "The Policemans' Lot." In C. *Urban Policing,* edited by Beverly Hills Hahn.: Sage.

Bordua, D., and A. J. Reiss, Jr. 1966. "Command, Control and Charisma: Reflections on Police Bureaucracy." *American Journal of Sociology* 72 (July): 68–76.

———. 1967. "Law Enforcement." In P. Lazarsfeld, W. Sewell and H. Wilensky *The Uses of Sociology,* edited by New York: Basic Books.

Bourdieu, P. 1977. *Outline of a Theory of Practice.* Cambridge, Eng.: Cambridge University Press.

———. *Language and Symbolic Power.* Cambridge, England: Polity.

Brantingham, P.L., and P.J. Brantingham, ed. 1990. *Environmental Criminology.* Prospect Heights, Ill. Waveland Press.

Brogdan, M., and C. Shearing. 1993. *Policing for a New South Africa.* London: Routledge & Kegan Paul.

Bronick, M.G. 1989. "The Federal Bureau of Prisons' Experience with Privatization." Unpublished paper. U.S. Bureau of Prisons, Washington, D.C.

Brown, L.P. 1989. "Community Policing: A Practical Guide for Police Officials" In *Perspectives on Policing.* Washington, D.C.: U.S. Government Printing Office.

Bureau of Justice Statistics. 1988. *Report to the Nation on Crime and Justice.* 2d ed. Washington, D.C.: U.S. Department of Justice

Brown, M. 1981. *Working the Street.* New York: Russell Sage.

Burke, K. 1962. *A Grammar of Motives and a Rhetoric of Motives.* Cleveland: Meridian.

Cain, M. 1973. *Society and the Policeman's Role.* London: Routledge & Kegan Paul.

Cain, M. 1979. "Trends in the Sociology of Police Work." *International Journal of the Sociology of Law* 7: 143–67.

Carson W. G. O. 1970. "White Collar Crime and the Enforcement of Factory Legislation" *British Journal of Criminology* 10:383–98.

Carte, G., and E. Carte. 1977. "August Vollmer." In *Pioneers in Policing,* edited by J. Slead. Montclair, N. G.: Patterson Smith.

Chatterton, M. 1987, "Assessing Police Effectiveness: Future Prospects" *British Journal of Criminology* 20: 80–86.

Chatterton, M., and Paula Whitehead. 1997. "Supermanagement: The Role of BCU Commanders." Unpublished paper, Fielding Centre, University of Manchester.

Clarke, R. V. 1980. "Situational Crime Prevention: Theory and Practice." *British Journal of Criminology* 20: 136–47.

———. 1992. *Situational Crime Prevention: Successful Case Studies.* New York: Harrow and Heston.

Clarke, R., and M. Hough, eds. 1980. *The Effectiveness of the Police.* Aldershot, Eng.: Gower.

Cohen S. 1985. *Visions of Social Control.* Cambridge, England: Polity.

Colby, P.W. 1995. *The Encyclopedia of Police Science,* 2d ed., S.V. "contract police."

Cory, B. 1979. "Police for Hire: Fear Pays a Dividend to Those Who Guard". *Police.* 2 (September 1979):39–45

Corwin, M. 1996. *The Killing Season: A Summer Inside an LAPD Homicide Division.* New York: Fawcett.

Crank, J. 1994. "Watchman and Community: Myth and Institutionalization in Policing," *Law and Society Review* 28: 325–51.

————. 1997. Understanding Police Culture. Cincinnati: Anderson.

Critchley, T. 1978. *A History of Police in England and Wales 1990– 1966.* London: Constable.

Cunningham, W.C., and T.H. Taylor, 1985a *The Hallcrest Report: Private Security and Police in America,* Portland, Ore.: Chancellor.

Cunningham, W.C., J. Strauchs, and C. Van Meter 1990. *The Hallcrest Report II: Private Security Trends, 1970–2000* Stoneham, Mass.: Butterworth-Heineman.

————. 1991. *Private Security: Patterns and Trends.* Washington, D.C.: National Institute of Justice.

————. 1985b. In *Crime and Protection in America: A Study of Private Security and Law Enforcement Resources and Relationships,* edited by D. Ford. Washington, D.C.: National Institute of Justice, 1985.

Davis, M. 1992. *City of Quartz.* New York: Random House.

Davis, M. R. Lundman, and R. Martinez, Jr. 1991. "Private Corporate Justice: Store Police, Shoplifters, and Civil Recovery." *Social Problems,* 38:395–408.

Deakin, T.J. 1988. *Police Professionalism: The Renaissance of American Law Enforcement.* Springfield, Ill. Charles C. Thomas.

Del Carmen, R. 1991. *Police Civil Liabilities.* Saddle River, N.J.: Prentice Hall.

Demsetz, H. 1970. "The Private Production of Public Goods." *Journal of Law and Economics* 13 (October 1970):293–306

Dentzer, S. 1996. "Social Security: Hot Summer Sequel." *U.S. News & World Report,* 8, July 49.

Draper H. 1979. *Private Police.* Middlesex, Eng.: Penguin.

Drucker, P.F. 1988. "The Non-Profits' Quiet Revolution" *Wall Street Journal,* 8 September.

————. 1995. "*Really* Reinventing Government" *Atlantic Monthly,* February, 49–61.

Dubos, R. 1968. *So Human an Animal.* New York: Scribners. "Policing for Profit: Welcome to the New World of Private Security," 1997. *Economist,* 19, April.

Durkheim, E. 1964. *The Rules of Sociological Method.* Glencoe, Ill.: Free Press.

————. 1961. *The Elementary Forms of Religious Life.* New York: Collier/ Macmillan.

Eck, J. 1983. *Solving Crimes.* Washington D.C.: Police Foundation.

Edelman, M. 1988. *Constructing the Political Spectacle.* Chicago: University of Chicago Press.

Elliott, N. "The Growth of Privatized Policing." *Freeman* 41 (February 1991). 41–43.

Emsley, Clive, 1996. *The English Police.* 21 ed. Addison-Wesley Longman.

Ericson, R. V.. 1981. *Making Crime.* Toronto: Butterworths.

————. 1982. *Reproducing Order.* Toronto: University of Toronto Press.

————. 1989, "Patrolling the Facts: Secrecy and Publicity in Policework" *British Journal of Sociology* 40 (June): 205–26

————. 1991 "Mass Media, Crime, Law, and Justice" *British Journal of Criminology* 31 (summer): 219–49.

————. 1992. "The Division of Labour and the Concept of Security." Unpublished paper. University of Toronto, Centre of Criminology.

Ericson, R. V., and K. Haggerty. 1997. *Policing the Risk Society.* Toronto: University of Toronto Press.

Ericson, R. V. P. Baranek, and J. Chan. 1989 *Negotiating Control: A study of News Sources.* Toronto: University of Toronto Press.

Etzioni, A. 1988. *The Moral Dimension.* New York: Free Press.

———. 1993. *The Spirit of Community.* New York: Crown.

Amitai Etzioni et al. (30 signatories) 1991. "The Responsive Communitarian Platform: Rights and Responsibilities." Unpublished document.

Feeley, M. 1970. "Coercion and Compliance: A New Look at an Old Problem." *Law and Society Review* 4: 505–19.

Feeley, M., and J. Simon. 1994. "Actuarial Justice: The Emerging New Criminal Law." in *The Futures of Criminology,* edited by D. Nelken. London: Sage Ltd.

Fielding, N. 1988. *Joining Forces.* London: Routledge, Kegan Paul.

———. 1996. *Community Policing.* Oxford: Oxford University Press

Fielding, N. 1991. *The Police and Social Conflict: Rhetoric and Reality.* London and Atlantic Highlands, N.J.: Athlone Press.

Fixler, P., Jr., and R. W. Poole, Jr. 1998 "Can the Police Be Privatized?", In *Privatizing the United States Justice System: Police, Adjudication, and Corrections Services from The Private Sector,* edited by G. Boroman, S. Haki and P. Seidenstat Jefferson, N.C. Mc Farland & Co. (Annals 498:.)

Flusty, S. 1994. *The Proliferation of Interdictory Space and the Erosion and Spatial Justice.* Los Angeles. Los Angeles Forum for Architecture and Urban Design.

Fogelson, R. 1977. *Big City Police.* Cambridge, Mass.: Harvard University Press.

Foucault, M. 1977. *Discipline and Punish.* New York: Pantheon.

Forst, B., J. Lucianovic, and S. Cox. 1977. *What Happens After Arrest?* Washington, D.C. Institute for Law and Social Research.

Frank, R. 1988. *Passions within Reason: The Strategic Role of the Emotions* New York: Norton.

Friedman, M. 1953. "The Methodology of Positive Economics." In *Essays in Positive Economics,* edited by Milton Friedman. Chicago: University of Chicago Press.

Fukuyama, F. 1995. *Trust: The Social Virtues and the Creation of Prosperity.* New York: Free Press.

Fyfe, J. 1988. "Police Use of Deadly Force: Research and Reform." *Justice Quarterly* 5: 165–205.

Fyfe, Nicholas R. 1995. "Policing the City." *Urban Studies* 32 (May): 759–78.

Gates, W. 1996. *The Road Ahead.* New York: Penguin.

Geller, W., and N. Morris, 1992, "Federal-State Relations." In *Modern Policing.* Vol. 15 of *Crime and Justice: A Review of Research,* edited by N. Morris and M. Tonry. Chicago: University of Chicago Press.

Gergen, D. 1996. "Our Most Valued Right." *U. S. News and World Report,* 24 June, 72.

Gergen, K. 1991. *The Saturated Self.* New York: Basic Books.

Gest, T. 1995. "Street Crime: People Fight Back." *U.S. News and World Report,* 15 April.

Gill M., and J. Hart. 1997. "Exploring Investigative Policing." *British Journal of Criminology* 37 (autumn):549–67.

Glendon, M. A. 1991. *Rights Talk: The Impoverishment of Political Discourse*. New York: Free Press.

Goffman, E. 1959. *The Presentation of Self in Everyday Life*. New York: Doubleday Anchor.

———. 1974. *Frame Analysis*. New York: Basic Books.

———. 1983a. "Felicity's Condition." *American Journal of Sociology* 89(1) 1–53.

———. 1983b. "The Interaction Order," *American Sociological Review* 48: 1–17.

Goldstein, H. 1977. *Policing a Free Society*. Mass: Ballinger.

———. 1990. *Problem-Oriented Policing*. New York: McGraw-Hill.

Goodhall, C. 1989. *Casing the Promised Land*. Carbondale, Ill.: Southern Illinois University Press.

Gore, A. 1993. *From Red Tape to Results: Creating a Government That Works Better and Costs Less*. Washington, D.C.: U.S. Government Printing Office.

———. 1995. *Common Sense Government Works Better and Costs Less*. Washington, D.C.: U.S. Government Printing Office.

Gusfield. J. 1966. *Symbolic Politics*. Urbana: University of Illinois Press.

Guyot, D. 1991. *Policing as Though People Matter*. Philadelphia: Temple University Press.

Hage, D. W. Cohen, and R. F. Black. 1995. "Reversing the Tide: Washington Turns to Privatization to Help Reduce the Budget Deficit." *U.S. News & World Report,* 3 April, 42–46.

Hakim, S. and A. J. Buck. 1991. *Residential Security: The Hakim-Buck Study on Suburban Alarm Effectiveness*. Philadelphia: Temple University Press.

Hakim, S. G.F. Rengert, and Y. Shachmurove. 1996. "Estimation of Net Benefits of Residential Electronic Security." *Justice Quarterly,* 13 (March):153–70.

Hart, J. W. 1951. *The British Police*. London: Allen and Unwin.

Hart J. W. 1956, "The Reform of Borough Police: 1835–1856." *English Historical Review* 70 (July):411–27.

Heath, T. 1996. "Games End, Finger-Pointing Begins: ACOG Official Says Organizers and Police 'Lost Control of the Streets.'" *Washington Post,* 6 August.

Heimer, C. 1985a. *Reactive Risk and Rational Action*. Berkeley: University of California Press.

———. 1985b. "Social Structure, Psychology and the Estimation of Risk." In *Annual Review of Sociology,* edited by R. Turner. Vol. 14 491–519. Palo Alto, Calif.: Annual Review Press.

Hilke, J. 1992. *Competition in Government Financed Services*. New York: Praeger.

Hirschman A. 1979. *Exit, Voice and Loyalty*. Princeton: Princeton University Press.

Hodson, R. 1996. "Dignity in the Workplace under Participative Management." *American Sociological Review* 61:719–38.

Holdaway, Simon, ed. 1979. *British Policing*. London: E. A. Arnold.

———. 1983. *Inside the British Police*. Oxford: Blackwells. 1983

Hough, J. M. 1980a. "Managing with Less Technology." *British Journal of Criminology*. 20:344–57.

———. 1980b. *Uniformed Police Work and Management Technology*. Home Office. Research and Planning Unit Paper 1. London: HM Stationery Office.

Howson, G. 1970. *The Thief-Taker General*. London: Hutchinson.

Hughes, E. C. 1971. *The Sociological Eye*. Chicago: Aldine.

Hunt, R. and J. Magenau. 1993. *Power and the Police Chief*. Thousand Oaks, Calif.: Sage.

Jackall, R. 1988. *Moral Mazes* New York: Oxford University Press.

——— 1997. *Wild Cowboys*. Cambridge, Mass. Harvard University Press.

Jacobs, J. 1983. *Encyclopedia of Crime and Justice,* S.V. "police: private police and security forces."

Johnston, L. 1992. *The Rebirth of Private Policing*. London: Routledge & Kegan Paul.

Jones, T. and T. Newburn. 1998. *Private Security and Public Policing*. Oxford: Clarendon Press.

Kakalik, J. S., and S. Wildhorn. 1972. *Private Security in the United States* ["The Rand Report"]. 5 vols. Washington, D.C.: National Institute of Law Enforcement and Criminal Justice.

———. 1977. *The Private Police: Security and Danger*. New York: Crane, Russak.

Kellermann, A. L., F. P. Rivara, N.B. Rushforth, J.G. Banton, D.T. Reay, J. T. Francisco, A. B. Locci, J. Prodzinski, B. B. Hackman, and G. Somes. 1993. "Gun Ownership as a Risk Factor for Homicide in the Home." *New England Journal of Medicine*. 329 (7 October):1084–91.

Kellermann, A. L. F. P. Rivara, G. Somes, D. T. Reay, J. Francisco, J. G. Banton, J. Prodzinski, C. Fligner, and B. B. Hackman. 1992. "Suicide in the Home in Relation to Gun Ownership." *New England Journal of Medicine*. 327 (13 August):467–72.

Kelling, G., and C. Coles. 1996. *Fixing Broken Windows: Restoring Order in American Cities*. New York: Free Press.

Kelling, G. A. Pate, D. Dieckman, and C. Brown. 1974. *The Kansas City Preventive Patrole Experiment: A Summary Report*. Washington, D.C.: Police Foundation.

Kelsen, H. 1961. *A General Theory of Law and the State*. New York: Russell and Russell.

Keynes, J. M. 1973. *The General Theory of Employment, Interest and Money*. New York: Harcourt Brace, 1936. Reprint, Cambridge, England: Cambridge University Press

Kleck G. 1991. *Point Blank*. Hawthorne, N.Y.: Aldine.

Klockars, C. 1985. *The Idea of Police*. Newbury Park, Calif.: Sage.

———. 1995. "The Dirty Harry Problem." In *The Police and Society: Touchstone Readings,* edited by V. E. Kappeler. Prospect Heights, Ill.: Waveland Press.

Kraska, P., and V. Kappeler. 1997. "Militarizing the American Police: The Rise and Normalization of Paramilitary Units." *Social Problems* 44:1–18.

Laband, D. and J. P. Sophocleus. 1992. "An Estimate of Resource Expenditures on

Transfer Activities in the United States." *Quarterly Journal of Economics.* 107:959–83.

LaFave, W. 1967. *Arrest.* Boston: Little, Brown.

Landes, W. M., and R. A. Posner. 1975. "The Private Enforcement of Law." *Journal of Legal Studies.* 1:1–46.

Lane, R. 1967. *Policing the City.* Cambridge, Mass.: Harvard University Press.

Lipsky, M. 1980. *Street-Level Bureaucrats.* New York: Russell Sage.

Lopez de Solanes, F., A. Shleifer, and R. Vishny. 1995. "Privatization in the United States." National Bureau of Economic Research, working paper number 5113.

Luhmann, N. 1993. *Risk: A Sociological Theory.* Hawthorne, N.Y.: Aldine/DeGruyter.

Lyon, D. 1994. *The Electronic Eye: the Rise of Surveillance Society.* Minneapolis: University of Minnesota Press.

Macauley, S. 1963. "Non-contractual Relations in Business: A Preliminary Study." *American Sociological Review* 28 (February):55–69.

Maguire, E. 1997. "Structural Change in Large Municipal Police Organizations During the Community Policing Era." *Justice Quarterly* 14:547–76.

Manning, P. K. 1977. *Police Work: The Social Organization of Policing.* Cambridge, Mass.: MIT Press.

Manning, P. K. 1979. *The Narcs' Game.* Cambridge, Mass.: MIT Press.

———. 1988. *Symbolic Communication.* Cambridge, Mass.: MIT Press.

———. 1992. "The Police and Information Technologies." In *Modern Policing.* Vo. 15 of *Crime and Justice: A Review of Research,* edited by M. Tonry and N. Morris Chicago: University of Chicago Press.

———. 1993. "Community Policing". In *Critical Issues in Policing.* 2d ed., edited by R. G. Dunham and G. Alpert. Prospect Heights, Ill: Waveland Press.

——— 1994a. "Economic Rhetoric and Police Reform" in *The Police and Society,* edited by V. Kappeler. Prospect Heights, Ill: Waveland Press.

———.1994b. "The Police: Mandate, Strategies, and Appearance." In *The Policy and Society,* edited by V. Kappeler. Prospect Heights, Ill.: Waveland Press.

———1994c. "Violence and Symbolic Violence." In *The Police and Society,* edited by V. Kappeler. Prospect Heights, Ill: Waveland Press.

———1996. "Dramaturgy, Politics and the Axial Media Event." *Sociological Quarterly.* 37:101–18.

———. 1997. *Police Work.* 2 ed. Prospect Heights, Ill: Waveland Press.

Manning, P. K., and K. Hawkins. 1987. "Police Decision-Making." In *The Future of Police Research,* edited by M. Weatheritt. Aldershot, Eng.: Gower.

Manning, P. K., and L. J. Redlinger. 1977. "Working Basis of Corruption." In *Drugs and Society,* edited by P. Rock. Rutgers, N. J.: Transaction/Society Books.

Manning, Phillip. 1993. *Erving Goffman and Modern Sociology.* Palo Alto, Calif.: Stanford University Press.

Mansbridge, J. 1990. *Beyond Self-Interest.* Chicago: University of Chicago.

Martin, J. 1996. "Who Killed Modern Manners?" *Responsive Community.* 6 (spring):50–57.

Martin, S. 1990. *Progress in Policing*. Washington, D. C.: Police Foundation.

Martin, S. "Drivel." 1997. *New Yorker,* 22 and 29 December, 138.

Marx, G. 1988. *Undercover.* Berkeley: University of California Press.

Mastrofski, S. 1988. "Community Policing as Reform." In *Community Policing,* edited by J. Greene and S. Mastrofski New York: Praeger.

Mastrofski, S. 1990. "The Prospects of Change in Police Patrol: A Decade in Review." *American Journal of Police* 9 (3):1–79.

Matthews, R., ed. 1989. *Privatizing Criminal Justice*. London: Sage, Ltd.

Mawby, R. 1997. "Managing Media and Public Relations in the Police Service." *Police Research and Management* 1 (autumn):41–59.

McCrie, R. D. 1988. "The Development of the U.S. Security Industry." In *The Annals of the American Academy of Political and Social Science: The Private Security Industry: Issues and Trends,* edited by I. A. Lipman (Newbury Park, CA: Sage), Volume 498 (July 1988): 23–33.

McDonald, D. C. 1992. "Private Penal Institutions." In *Crime and Justice: A Review of Research,* edited by M. Tonry. Vol. 16, 361–419. Chicago: University of Chicago Press.

Mead, G. H. 1934. *Mind, Self and Society*. Chicago: University of Chicago Press.

Meyer, J., and C. Rowan. 1977. "Institutionalized Organization: Formal Structure as Myth and Ceremony." *American Journal of Sociology* 83:340–63.

Meyrowitz, J. 1985. *No Sense of Place*. New York: Oxford University Press.

Miethe, T. D. 1991. "Citizen-Based Crime Control Activity and Victimization Risks: An Examination of Displacement and Free-Rider Effects." *Criminology* 29:419–40.

Miller, W. 1977. *Police and Bobbies*. Chicago: University of Chicago Press.

Miller, J. 1997 *Search and Destroy*. Cambridge, Eng.: CUP.

Mills, C. W. 1960. *The Sociological Imagination*. New York: Grove Press.

Monkkonen, E. 1981. *Police in Urban America*. Cambridge, Eng.: Cambridge University Press.

———. 1992. "History of Urban Police." In *Modern Policing*. Vol. 15 of *Crime and Justice: An Annual Review of Research,* edited by M. Tonry and N. Morris. Chicago: University of Chicago Press.

Moore, M., and R. Trojanowicz. 1988. "Corporate Strategies for Policing." *Perspectives on Policing,* no. 4. U.S. Department of Justice. National Institute of Justice.

Moore, M., R. Trojanowicz, and G. Kelling, 1988. "Crime and Policing" *Perspectives on Policing,* no. 3. U.S. Department of Justice. National Institute of Justice.

Moore, M. 1995. *Creating Public Value*. Cambridge Mass.: Harvard University Press.

Moran, J. 1995. "Privatizing Criminal Justice." Paper delivered at the Futures Conference on Privatizing Criminal Justice: Public and Private Partnerships, 13–15 March, University of Illinois at Chicago.

Morn F. 1992. *The Eye That Never Sleeps*. Bloomington: Indiana University Press.

Mueller, D. 1989. *Public Choice*. 2d ed. Cambridge, Eng.: Cambridge University Press.

Nalla, M., and G. Newman. 1991. Public versus Private Control: A Reassessment. *Journal of Criminal Justice* 19:537–47.

———. 1993. *A Primer on Private Security.* Albany, N.Y.: Harrow and Heston.

Newman, B. 1997. "Dutch Are Invading JFK Arrivals Building and None Too Soon." *Wall Street Journal,* 13 May.

Nozick, R. 1974. *Anarchy, State and Utopia.* Oxford: Blackwell.

Nuzum, M. 1998. "The Commercialization of Justice." *The Critical Criminologist* 8:(summer) 1, 5–9.

Office of International Criminal Justice. 1995. "Readings." Ninth Annual Futures Conference on Privatization in Criminal Justice: Public and Private Partnerships, 13–15 March, University of Illinois at Chicago.

Office of Management and Budget. 1955. Circular A-76. Washington, D.C.: U.S. Government Printing Office.

O'Malley P. 1996. "Policing, Politics and Postmodernity," Paper presented to Law and Society Meetings, Glasgow, Strathclyde University, July 13–15.

Parsons, T. 1936. *The Structure of Social Action.* New York: McGraw-Hill.

Pate A. M., M. A. Wycoff, W. G. Skogan, and L. W. Sherman. 1985. *Reducing Fear of Crime in Houston and Newark: A Summary Report.* Washington, D.C.: Police Foundation.

Pepinsky, H. 1980. *Crime Control Strategies.* New York: Oxford University Press.

Perkins, C. and P. Klaus. 1996. "Criminal Victimization 1994," *Bureau of Justice Statistics Bulletin.* Washington, D.C.: U.S. Department of Justice.

Phillips, L. 1993. "Economic Perspectives on Criminality" An Eclectic View. In *The Socio-Economics of Crime and Justice,* edited by Brian Forst. Armonk, N.Y.: M. E. Sharpe.

Police Review, 1989. 13 January, 65.

Poole, R. W., Jr. 1978. *Cutting Back City Hall.* New York: Free Press, 1978.

Posner, R. A. 1972. *Economic Analysis of Law.* Boston: Little, Brown.

———. 1981. *The Economics of Justice.* Cambridge, Mass.: Harvard University Press.

Poster, M. 1990. *The Mode of Information.* Chicago: University of Chicago Press.

President's Crime Commission. 1967. *The Challenge of Crime in a Free Society.* Washington D.C.: U.S. Government Printing Office.

Powell, M., S. Horwitz, and C. Thompson. 1997. "Problems in D.C. Police Department Festered for Decades." *Washington Post,* 12 October.

Pririe, M. 1988. *Privatization.* Aldershot, Eng.: Wildwood House.

"Private Firms Take Over Public Functions: Germany, Switzerland." 1980. *Urban Innovation Abroad:*4 (September):1.

Punch, M. 1979. *Policing the Inner City.* London: Macmillan.

Putnam, R. 1991. "Bowling Alone" Unpublished essay.

Radzinowicz. L. *A History of English Criminal Law 1948–1962.* 4 vols. London: Stevens.

Radzinowicz, L. 1948–66. *History of the English Criminal Law.* 4 vol. New York: Macmillan.

Rau, C. 1989. "Security Industry Faces a Control Crisis." *The Age,* 16 October.

Reaves, B. 1996. *Local Police Departments, 1993*. Washington, D.C.: Bureau of Justice Statistics.

Reaves, B., and Z. Smith. 1996 *Sheriff's Departments, 1993*. Washington, D.C. : Bureau of Justice Statistics.

Reiner, R. 1978. *The Blue-Coated Worker*. Cambridge: Cambridge University Press.

————.1991. *Chief Constables*. Oxford: Oxford University Press.

————. 1992. *The Politics of the Police*. 2d ed. Brighton, Eng.: Wheatsheaf.

Reiss. Albert J., Jr. 1971. *Police and the Public*. New Haven: Yale University Press.

————. 1974. "Discretionary Justice." In *Handbook of Criminology*, edited by D. Glaser Chicago: Rand McNally.

————. 1983. "Policing Organizational Life." In *Control in the Police Organization*, edited by M. Punch Cambridge, Mass.: MIT Press.

————. 1984. "Selecting Strategies of Control over Organizational Lie." In *Enforcing Regulation*, edited by K. Hawkins and J. Thomas. Boston: Kluwer-Nijhoff.

————. 1988. *Private Employment of Public Police*. Washington, D.C.: National Institute of Justice.

————. 1992a. "A Theory of the Police." Presentation to American Society of Criminology, November Phoenix, Arizona.

————. 1992b. "Twentieth Century Policing." In *Modern Policing*. Vol. 15 of *Crime and Justice: A Review of Research* edited by M. Tonry and N. Morris. Chicago: University of Chicago Press.

————. 1995. "Crime Prevention in Urban Communities." *Annales Internationale de Criminologie* 30 (1), nos. 1 and 2.

————. and D. Bordua. 1967. "Environment and Organization." In *The Police: Six Sociological Essays*, edited by D. Bordua. New York: J Wiley.

Reppetto, T. 1978. *The Blue Parade*. New York: Macmillan.

Rheingold, H. 1992 *Virtual Communities*. New York: Simon and Schuster.

Ritzer. G. 1992. The *MacDonaldization of Society*. Thousand Oaks, Calif.: Pine Forge Press.

Rock, P. 1983. "Law, Order and Power in the Late Seventeenth and Early Eighteenth Century," In *Social Control and the State*, edited by S. Cohen and A. Scull. Oxford, Eng.: Martin Robertson.

Rosenbaum, D., ed. 1986. *Community Crime Prevention*. Beverly Hills, Calif.: Sage.

————, ed. 1994. *The Challenge of Community Policing*. Newbury Park, Calif.: Sage.

Rosenbloom, D. H. 1998. "Constitutional Problems for the New Public Management in the United States." In *Current Public Policy Issues: The 1998 Annals*, edited by Khai Thai and Rosalyn Y. Carter. Boca Raton, Fl.

Rubinstein, J. 1973. *City Police*. New York: Farrar, Straus and Giroux.

Samuelson, P. 1947. *Foundations of Economic Analysis*. Cambridge, Mass.: Harvard University Press.

———— 1954. "The Pure Theory of Public Expenditure." *Review of Economics and Statistics* 36 (November):387—90.

Sarbin, T., ed. 1997. *Vision 2021: Security Issues for the Next Quarter Century.* Conference Proceedings BDM Headquarters MacLean, VA, June 1996 sponsored by Defense Personnel Security Research Center (PERSEREC) and Security Policy Board Staff.

Sashkin, M., and K. J. Kiser 1993. *Putting Total Quality, Management to Work.* San Francisco: Berrett-Koehler.

Saunders, P. and C. Harris. 1990. "Privatization and the Consumer." *Sociology* 24:57–75.

Savas, E. S. 1982. *Privatizing the Public Sector.* Chatham, N.J.: Chatham House.

———. 1987. *Privatization: The Key to Better Government.* Chatham, N.J.: Chatham House.

Scheingold, S. 1984. *The Politics of Law and Order.* New York: Longman.

———. 1991. *The Politics of Street Crime.* Philadelphia: Temple University Press.

Scheptycki, J. 1996. "Transnational Policing and the Makings of the Postmodern State." *British Journal of Criminology*

———, ed. Forthcoming. *Transnational Policing.* London, Eng.: Routledge.

Senna, J. J., and L. J. Siegel. 1993. *Introduction to Criminal Justice.* 6th ed. Minneapolis: West.

Shapiro, S. 1987. "The Social Organization of Interpersonal Trust." *American Journal of Sociology* 93:623–58.

Shearing, C., and P. Stenning 1981. "Modern Private Security: Its Growth and Implications." in *Crime and Justice: An Annual Review of Research,* edited by M. Tonry and N. Morris. Vol. 3. Chicago: University of Chicago Press.

———. 1983. "Private Security—Implications for Social Control." *Social Problems* 30:493–506.

———, eds. 1987. *Private Security.* Newbury Park, Calif.: Sage.

Shearing, C. 1984. Dial-A-Cop. Toronto: Centre for Criminology.

———. 1992. "The Relation Between Public and Private Policing." In *Modern Policing.* Vol. 15 of *Crime and Justice: An Annual Review of Research* edited by M. Tonry and N. Morris. Chicago: University of Chicago Press.

Sherman, L. W., 1986, "Policing Communities: What Really Works?" In *Crime and the Community.* Vol 20 of *Crime and Justice:* A Review of Research, edited by A. J. Reiss, Jr. and M. Tonry. Chicago: University of Chicago Press.

———. 1992. "Attacking Crime: Policing and Crime Control." In *Modern Policing.* Vol. 15 of *Crime and Justice: A Review of the Research* edited by M. Tonry and N. Morris. Chicago: University of Chicago Press.

———.1995. "The Police." In *Crime,* edited by J. Q. Wilson and J. Petersilia, 327–48. San Francisco: ICS Press.

Sherman, L. W. and the National Advisory Commission on Higher Education for Police Officers. 1978. *The Quality of Police Education.* San Francisco: Josey-Bass.

Shils, E. 1956, *The Torment of Secrecy.* Glencoe, Ill.: Free Press.

Shook, Howard. "Security's Positive Return." *Security Management* (October 1997), pp 7–10

Silbey, S. 1997. "Let Them Eat Cake: Globalization, Postmodern Colonialism and the Possibilities of Justice." *Law and Society Review* 31:297–35.

Silver, A. 1967, "The Demand for Order in Civil Society," In *The Police: Six Sociological Essays,* edited by D. Bordua. New York: Wiley.

Simon, D. 1992. *Homicide.* Boston: Houghton Mifflin.

Skogan W. 1988. "Community Organizations and Crime." In *Crime and Justice: A Review of Research,* edited by M. Tonry and N. Morris. Vol. 8. Chicago: University of Chicago Press.

———— 1991. *Disorder and Decline.* Berkeley: University of California Press.

———— 1996. *Annual Report of CAPs.* Chicago.

Skogan, W., and S. Harnett. 1997. *Community Policing, Chicago Style.* Chicago: University of Chicago Press.

Skolnick, J., and J. J. Fyfe. 1993. *Above the Law: Police and the Excessive Use of Force.* New York: Free Press.

Skolnick, J. 1994. *Justice without Trial: Law Enforcement in Democractic Society.* 3d ed. New York: Macmillan.

————1996. *Justice without Trial.* New York: Wiley.

Smith, A. [1776] 1937. *An Inquiry into the Nature and Causes of the Wealth of Nations.* Reprint, New York: Modern Library.

————. [1759] 1966. *The Theory of Moral Sentiments.* Reprint, New York: Kelleyo

Smith D. and Gray 1986. *Police and People in London.* London: Policy Studies Institute.

South, Nigel, 1988. *Policing for Profit.* London: Sage, Ltd.

————. 1989. "Reconstructing Policing." In *Privatizing Criminal Justice,* edited by R. Matthews. London: Sage, Ltd.

Sparrow, M. K., M. H. Moore, and D. M. Kennedy. 1990. *Beyond 911: A New Era for Policing.* New York: Basic Books.

Spitzer S., and A. Scull. 1977a. "Privatization and Capitalist Development: The Case of Private Police." *Social Problems* 25:18–29.

————. 1977b. "Social Control in Historical Perspective." In *Corrections and Punishment* edited by D. Greenburg. Beverly Hills, Calif.: Sage.

Stead, J., ed. 1977. *Pioneers in Policing.* Montclair, N.J.: Patterson Smith.

Steel, D., and D. Heald. 1984. *"The New Agenda" in Privatizing Public Services.* London: Royal Institute of Public Administration.

Stengel, R. 1996. "Bowling Together." *Time,* 22 July, 35–36.

Stevens, J. 1989. *Encyclopedia of Police Science,* S.V. "Computer Technology."

Stewart, J. K. 1985. "Public Safety and Private Police." *Public Administration Review* 45 (November): 758–65.

Surette, R. 1991. *Media, Crime and Criminal Justice.* Monterey, Calif.: Brooks Cole.

Sviridoff, M. "The Seeds of Urban Revival." 1984. *The Public Interest* no. 114 (winter 1994):82–103.

Thomas, R. J. 1994 *What Machines Can't Do.* Berkeley: University of California Press.

Thompson, J. 1967, *Organizations in Action.* New York: McGraw-Hill.

Tien, J., and K. Colton. 1979. "Police Command, Control, and Communications." In *What Works?* Law Enforcement Assistance Administration. Washington, D.C.: U.S. Government Printing Office.

Timm, H., and K. Christian. 1991. *Introduction to Security.* Pacific Grove, Calif.: Brooks-Cole.

Toch, H. 1997. "The Democratization of Policing in the United States: 1895–1973." *Police Forum* 7 (April):1–8.

Toronto Police Department. 1990. "1990 Environmental Assessment and Force Goals and Objectives for 1991."

Trojanowicz, R. et al., 1982. *An Evaluation of the Neighborhood Foot Patrol Program in Flint, Michigan.* East Lansing, Mich.: Michigan State University.

Tunnell, K. 1992. "Film at Eleven: Recent Developments in the Commodification of Crime." *Sociological Spectrum* 12:293–313.

Uchida, C.D. 1993. "The Development of the American Police: An Historical Overview." In *Critical Issues in Policing,* edited by R. G. Dunham and G. P. Alpert. 16–32. Prospect Heights, Ill. Waveland Press.

Van Maanen, J. 1974 "Working the Street." In *Prospects for Reform in Criminal Justice,* edited by H. Jacob. Beverly Hills, Calif.: Sage.

Voelker, A.M. 1996 "NYPD's APPL Program: A New Partnership." *FBI Law Enforcement Bulletin,* February, 1–4

Vollmer, A. 1971. *The Police and Modern Society.* Reprint, Montclair, N.J.: Patterson Smith.

Walker, S. 1977. *A Critical History of Police Reform: The Emergence of Professionalism.* Lexington, Mass: Heath, Lexington Books.

Walsh, W. 1985 "Patrol Ofifcers' Arrest Rates." *Justice Quarterly 2* (September):271–90.

Walsh, W. F., and E. J. Donovan. 1989. "Private Security and Community Policing: Evaluation and Comment." *Journal of Criminal Justice* 17 (1989), pp. 187–97

Wambaugh, Joseph. *The Blue Knight* (Boston: Little Brown, 1972).

Washington Post. 1996. Editorial, "Private Probes for Public Jobs," 7 July.

Warr, M. 1995. "Crime and the Fear of Crime." In *Criminology,* edited by J. Sheley. Belmont, Calif.: Wadsworth.

Weber, M. 1949. *Methodology in the Social Sciences.* Glencoe, Ill.: Free Press.

Weber, M. 1954. *On Law in Economy and Society.* Edited by M. Rheinstein Cambridge, Mass.: Harvard University Press.

Weick, K. 1995. *Sense-Making in Organizations.* Thousand Oaks, Calif.: Sage.

Weisheit, R. D., N. Falcone, and L. Wells, 1996. *Crime and Policing in Rural and Small-Town America.* Prospect Heights, Ill: Waveland Press.

Westley, W. 1970. *Violence and the Police.* Cambridge, Mass.: MIT Press.

Wiley, N. 1994. *The Semiotic Self.* Chicago: University of Chicago Press.

Williams, H. 1991. "External Resources." In *Local Government Police Management,* edited by W. A. Geller. Washington, D.C.: International City Management Association.

Wilson, O. W. 1938. *Municipal Police Administration*. Chicago: International City Managers' Association. Subsequently published by McGraw-Hill, New York, 1950.

Wilson, J.Q. 1963. "The Police and their Problems." *Public Policy* 12:189–216.

———. 1968. *Varieties of Police Behavior*. Cambridge, Mass.: Harvard University Press.

———. 1993. *The Moral Sense*. New York: Free Press.

Wilson, J.Q., and G. Kelling. 1982. "The Police and Neighborhood Safety: Broken Windows." *Atlantic,* March, 29–38.

Wilson, W. J. 1987. *The Truly Disadvantaged: The Inner City, the Underclass, and Public Policy*. Chicago: University of Chicago Press.

Wolfe, Joan L., and J. Heaphy, eds. 1979. *Readings in Productivity in Policing*. Washington, D.C.: Police Foundation.

Index